CONTROLLED

CHAOS

Making Sense of

Junior High Ministry

"Learn to run a junior high group and you can rule the world."
—Bill Wennerholm

"Who wants to rule the world when you can run a junior high group!"
—Kurt Johnston

CONTROLLED

CHAOS

Making Sense of Junior High Ministry

Kurt Johnston

EMPOWERED® Youth Products
Standard Publishing
Cincinnati, Ohio

All Scripture quotations, unless otherwise indicated, are taken from the HOLY BIBLE, NEW INTERNATIONAL VERSION®. NIV®. Copyright © 1973, 1978, 1984 by International Bible Society. Used by permission of Zondervan Publishing House. All rights reserved.

Scripture quotations marked NLT are taken from the *Holy Bible*, New Living Translation, copyright © 1996. Used by permission of Tyndale House Publishers, Inc., Wheaton, Illinois 60189. All rights reserved.

Edited by Dale Reeves and Leslie Durden
Cover and inside design by Ahaa! Design/Dina Sorn

Library of Congress Cataloging-in-Publication Data:
Johnston, Kurt, 1966-
    Controlled chaos : making sense of junior high ministry / by Kurt Johnston.
      p. cm.
    "Empowered Youth Products."
    ISBN 0-7847-1254-9
    1. Church work with teenagers. 2. Junior high school students--Religious life. I. Title.
  BV1475.9 .J64 2001
  259'.23--dc21

                                      2001031066

Standard Publishing, Cincinnati, Ohio
A Division of Standex International Corporation.

08   07   06   05   04   03   02   01

7   6   5   4   3   2   1

DEDICATION

To Rick Williams, who has volunteered with junior high students in the same church for almost 20 years. While people like myself write books *about* junior high ministry, you quietly labor in the trenches *doing* junior high ministry.

ACKNOWLEDGMENTS

- A huge thanks to Doug Fields and the entire student ministries team at Saddleback. You're not only my colleagues, you're my friends.
- To Joe Schmaltz, Stephanie Flynn and Chris Tafalla. You are incredible partners.
- To Katie Edwards, Gregg Farah and Dean White. Thanks for the extra effort to help make sure this little book has maximum impact.
- To the volunteer team of Wildside. You are incredible! Thanks for sharing your ministry with me.
- To my family, Rachel, Kayla and Cole. You're all I need!

"Kurt Johnston's book gives me great hope for the church in the 21st century. I've observed this book 'lived out' through his fruitful ministry at Saddleback Church and I'm amazed at Kurt's leadership with junior high students and leaders. This is a man worth listening to! Anyone who works in the church knows that junior high may be the single most pivotal period for spiritual decisions in the lives of our children—that's why this book is so vital. If you're looking for a crazy new game or the latest junior high ministry fad, you've picked up the wrong book. If, instead, you want to build a healthy, purpose-driven ministry to junior high students, *Controlled Chaos* is your book. Digest it and learn from this veteran and your junior high students and their families will be blessed. . . . I know mine has."

— **Dr. Rick Warren,** senior pastor,
Saddleback Church

"Junior high is one of the most strategic ministries in the church, and Kurt has hit the nail on the head! His heart for junior high students, his experience as a leader and his light-hearted nature have combined for a great read."

— **John C. Maxwell,** founder,
The Injoy Group, www.injoy.com

"Kurt bleeds junior high ministry! In over 20 years of being in youth ministry, I've never met anyone who loves junior high ministry like he does. . . . what I've observed about our junior high ministry is that while God is busy doing the impossible, Kurt Johnston is leading his team of leaders to do the possible. He is a leader who is sensitive to what God wants to do with humanity and he is able to communicate that to junior high students and other leaders."

— **Doug Fields,** pastor to students, Saddleback Church,
author, *Purpose-Driven Youth Ministry*

"From the title page to the end of the book, it is obvious that Kurt Johnston knows junior high ministry. Packed with practical insight and sound content, this book has just the right blend of 'how-to,' 'how come?', 'why?' and even a little 'why not?' Kurt's conversational, down-to-earth writing style offers a high-octane mix of fun and wisdom to rev up junior high youth workers, both paid and volunteer! This would be a great resource to work through as an individual youth leader or as a ministry team. I highly recommend it."

— **Duffy Robbins,** associate professor of youth ministry,
Eastern College, St. Davids, PA

"In the search for a practical guide for junior high ministry, Kurt Johnston has struck the mother lode. No junior high worker, whether fresh rookie or experienced veteran, will view junior high ministry the same again."

— **Dr. Kara Eckman Powell,** assistant professor, Azusa Pacific University,
assistant junior high pastor, Lake Avenue Church

"Kurt Johnston has written a wonderfully practical guidebook for those of us who love junior highers. Reading this book feels like sitting down for a couple of hours with Kurt and gleaning from his years of experience—both good and bad! This book engagingly answers the oft-asked question, 'How do I do junior high ministry?'"

— **Mark Oestreicher,** vice president of ministry resources,
Youth Specialties

CONTENTS

F O R E W O R D

If you are reading this book, there is no question that you are an influential leader in your church. Junior high ministry is one of the most important and strategic ministries within the local church! Thank you for loving students during this difficult and awkward time in their lives. As a junior high leader, you are a minority within the body of Christ. Thank you! Thank you! Thank you for loving students and pointing them to God!

When junior high students get turned on to their faith, they are some of the most exciting and vivacious believers I've ever seen. They will bring their friends without embarrassment. They will serve without condition. They will follow without hesitation. And, they will live out their faith without compromise. I observe this firsthand from the junior high ministry within our church. This isn't fantasy; it's reality.

Obviously, God is at work behind any type of spiritual transformation in anyone's life, regardless of age. But what I've observed about our junior high ministry is that while God is busy doing the impossible, Kurt Johnston is leading his team of leaders to do the possible. He is a leader who is sensitive to what God wants to do with humanity and he is able to communicate that to junior high students and other leaders. I love what I see in Kurt's leadership and I'm honored to write this foreword. Because my space is limited, let me give you just four reasons why I'm so excited about this book.

First, Kurt bleeds junior high ministry! In over 20 years of being in youth ministry, I've never met anyone who loves junior high ministry like Kurt. He honestly doesn't want to do anything else with his life. I've seen higher paying job offers that he doesn't even look at because it would take him out of junior high ministry. You can learn from this type of passion and commitment.

Second, Kurt knows, understands and empathizes with junior high students! It's amazing, but these students know he likes them. I think I do a pretty good job pretending to like junior high students, but Kurt *actually* likes them. They know it too (I hear this all the time since my daughter is in junior high). You can learn from this type of loving leader.

Third, Kurt understands youth workers. He knows the "world" of the full-time junior high leader as well as the time issues facing the volunteer leader. You'll notice this immediately as Kurt's writing style is very practical. It's written from a guy who works in the trenches with junior high students every day and knows what you are going through. You can learn from this type of author.

Fourth, and most importantly, Kurt loves God. He has a rich relationship with God and his faith is authentic. I get to see it every day because we work together. He's not phony, unapproachable or arrogant. He's humble, genuine, and a lover of God, life and others. You can learn from this type of godly character.

I read a lot of youth ministry books and all the forewords seem to tell the reader how great the book is. Well, you'll find out about the book on your own. I want you to know that the words you're about to read are written from a man of God who is an outstanding youth worker. Kurt doesn't pretend to be an experienced writer; he's a youth worker who has been challenged to capture some of his learning so those who work with junior high students can glean from his experience. (Personally, I'd rather learn from this type of person than a writer who has little youth ministry experience.) Kurt wrote this book for those of you who love junior high students. I wish you could have felt some of his pain through his writing process—the late nights, the extra hours added to an already busy full-time junior high position, the multiple drafts, the edits from his caring wife Rachel, the discussions with every chapters . . . basically, all the "stuff" you never get to see when you read a book. Kurt pained over this book because he loves junior highers and he loves youth workers.

I want to encourage you to read this book with all your junior high leaders. Discuss it, make notes and work together to figure out how some of the principles will work in the context of your church. Kurt didn't write a lot about his junior high program because he doesn't want you to copy his program. He wants you to learn principles that you can adapt into your setting. Blessings to you as you read this book and learn from this leader.

A friend and fellow youth worker,
Doug Fields, pastor to students, Saddleback Church
Author, *Purpose-Driven Youth Ministry*

INTRODUCTION

"You're good. You could even be a real pastor," came the well-intentioned words from a pastor who had just heard me speak. If you've worked with junior high students for more than, say . . . an hour, you've probably heard similar comments. Early in my ministry career, I was often offended and discouraged by comments from people who just didn't seem to understand this thing called junior high ministry. However, this time was different. I walked away from my brief conversation with my common-sense impaired colleague with a renewed passion and calling.

Believe it or not, I actually enjoy the fact that junior high ministry is still a misunderstood arena. It reminds me of the importance of what I do. Junior highers are *real* people! They have real lives, real problems, real questions, real struggles, real relationships, real interests, real potential and are capable of living a life that reflects a real relationship with Jesus Christ—not to mention the fact that they are real fun!

This book is written to encourage those of you who work with young teens. Whether you are full-time, part-time or volunteer, I applaud you. You are neck-deep in waters that few people understand and even fewer dare enter. You *are* doing real ministry and you *are* making a real difference!

Here are a few suggestions to help you get the most out of this book:

First, I'm not an expert. I've been working with junior high students since 1988 when my best friend, Chris Schmaltz, and I managed to convince our church that we could be trusted to run a ten-week summer camp for the junior highers in our community. I've been a junior high pastor for quite a while, but I don't have all the answers, and neither will this book. What I do have is experience, insight and a desire to encourage other junior high youth workers.

Second, it's OK to disagree. If you agree with everything in this book, then I think you have no brain. As you read, you will most certainly question some of what I share. That's OK; in fact, that's good. It's not only good, it's biblical!

Next, be encouraged. Often, when I read something, I begin to feel as if I'm the only one out there who doesn't have it all together. As you work through this book, please understand that my ministry to junior highers has just as many holes in it as yours. I'm not doing everything I write about in these pages as well as I should be. It's also important to remember that all of us are at different stages in our ministry. Some of you are in large churches, but most aren't. Some have lots of help, but most don't. Some get paid, but most of you volunteer. Some of you have a budget, but for most of you the terms "junior high ministry" and "budget" are oxymorons. Here's the bottom line: Read this book through the filter of where your ministry is now and through the faith of where you want it to be.

Finally, do something with what you read. My bookshelf is full of four types of books: books for looks (commentaries, lexicons, book studies, etc.); books I mean to read but haven't gotten around to; books I've read but forgotten about; and books that I've read and actually implemented. I want you to read this book, but more importantly, I hope you will actually take bits and pieces of it and apply it to your own ministry. At the end of each chapter, you'll find a section entitled **Chew on This.** Work through the questions there as they apply to your ministry situation. Finally, each chapter concludes with a blank page entitled **Chaotic Thoughts.** I encourage you to record brain waves that have jumped out at you based on what you've just read and that are most relevant to your situation. From time to time you'll want to refer back to what you've written there. When we see each other here and there and you mention that you've read this book, I'll be flattered, but when you share what you've implemented, I'll be fulfilled.

"Well, there was no question now, we were entering uncharted territory. Junior high school was a whole new ball of wax." —Kevin Arnold; The Wonder Years

C H A P T E R   O N E

PUT YOURSELF IN THEIR SHOES
(Or better yet, put yourself back in your own)

How long has it been for you? Five, ten, fifteen years? It's been over twenty years since I strutted my stuff in the halls of Granada Middle School in La Mirada, California. A whole lot has changed since then. Jimmy Carter is no longer President of the United States, Starsky and Hutch have quit chasing bad guys and today girls don't think Shaun Cassidy is all that cute.

One of the keys to being an effective junior high youth worker is the willingness to journey back to your own early adolescence. It's natural that the older we get, the less we remember about our youth, but I think it's very important for junior high workers to revisit the past on a regular basis.

I absolutely loved junior high! Some of my fondest memories and funniest experiences happened during my three years at Granada. When I return to my junior high

BRAINWAVES

Whatever you remember about junior high, it's crucial that you do just that . . . remember junior high!

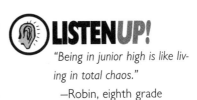

LISTENUP!

"Being in junior high is like living in total chaos."
—Robin, eighth grade

years, I end up with a smile on my face. You may feel differently. Your junior high memories may be less than pleasant. Whatever you remember about junior high, it's crucial that you do just that . . . remember junior high!

There are two steps you must take to put yourself into the shoes of a junior higher:

Step One:
RECOGNIZE THAT THE TIMES, THEY ARE A-CHANGIN'

Like I said, I graduated from eighth grade over 20 years ago. As much as this pains me, I'd like to give you a brief snapshot of what my world was like in 1980:

KURT'S JUNIOR HIGH WORLD CIRCA 1980

I had never seen a personal computer

Ronald Reagan was just heading into office

The Iran hostage crisis was in full swing

John Lennon was assassinated

Coal Miner's Daughter won the Oscar for best picture

The most popular show on TV was "Hill Street Blues"

My favorite band was Devo

The Pittsburgh Steelers won the Super Bowl

Every phone my family owned was connected to a cord

Needless to say, times have changed! The world is a different place today than it was when you and I were in junior high. You too can take a stroll down memory lane by visiting the website, www.info-please.com. This site can give you all the historical tidbits you could ever desire about any given year.

You may be asking, "Why should I take the time to look back at my junior high experience? What's that got to do with my ministry to students today?" Good questions! I don't have real clinical answers, just ones with common sense. By stepping back in time, you can begin to remember your journey forward that made you into the person you are today. Remembering what life was like for us helps us appreciate what life is like for today's young teenagers.

Let's take a brief look at what the world of a junior high student looks like now. This isn't an exhaustive study, but simply an exercise to help us appreciate what life is like for today's young teens.

JUNIOR HIGH WORLD CIRCA TODAY

Has grown up with the Internet

Doesn't remember the Gulf War

Probably owns his or her own cellphone or pager

Watches DVD instead of video

Downloads music instead of purchasing it

Spends more time in chat rooms than on the phone

Is already thinking about college

May have realized that college isn't as important as it used to be (may be making plans to launch an Internet startup instead!)

Is bombarded with twisted messages of sexuality

MTV

"Teen" prime-time shows

PG-13 movies

Increased sexuality in music lyrics

Lives in a world of increased violence

Probably attends a school that advocates tolerance but shuts down religious expression of any type

Is very interested in the spiritual realm

Wants to be like Kobe or Tiger, not Mike

Has never even seen an 8-track tape and maybe never listened to a cassette tape

You're probably not as far removed from your junior high years as I am, but it's easy to see just how quickly things change. I'd be willing to bet that even those of you in your late teens and early twenties can pinpoint a few changes in the above list from your junior high days. Take a few moments to think about how the world has changed since you were in eighth grade. Go ahead, put this book down and let yourself drift back.

Now that you feel really old, let me congratulate you. You have accomplished the first step in putting yourself in the shoes of today's junior high student. Hopefully that didn't hurt too much.

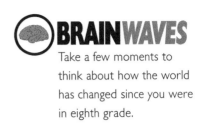

BRAINWAVES
Take a few moments to think about how the world has changed since you were in eighth grade.

STEP TWO:
Step Two:
RECOGNIZE THAT SOME THINGS NEVER CHANGE

"I was never like that," you say to yourself as a certain student pushes your button. Guess what? Yes you were! Chances are you were just like that. Although the world of a junior higher changes often, *who* a junior higher is has remained pretty much the same.

The second step to putting yourself into the shoes of junior highers is to recognize the various changes they are going through and remember that you once went through them too. Here's a brief look at the key areas of change or development that begin to occur in early adolescence. For a complete discussion, I recommend the book, *Junior High Ministry*, by Wayne Rice.

PHYSICAL DEVELOPMENT

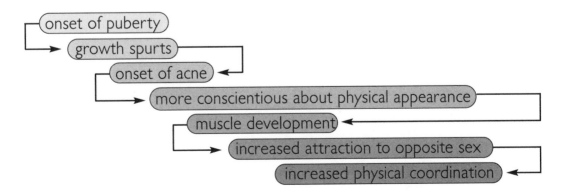

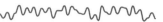

SOCIAL DEVELOPMENT

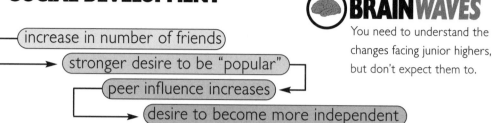

(increase in number of friends)

(stronger desire to be "popular")

(peer influence increases)

(desire to become more independent)

BRAINWAVES
You need to understand the
changes facing junior highers,
but don't expect them to.

INTELLECTUAL DEVELOPMENT

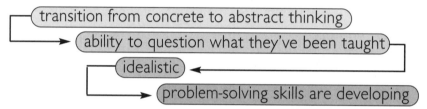

(transition from concrete to abstract thinking)

(ability to question what they've been taught)

(idealistic)

(problem-solving skills are developing)

EMOTIONAL DEVELOPMENT

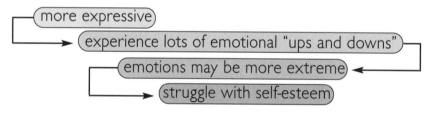

(more expressive)

(experience lots of emotional "ups and downs")

(emotions may be more extreme)

(struggle with self-esteem)

"Being in junior high is stress-ful, but I like it because it's always a new experience."
—Luke, seventh grade

SPIRITUAL DEVELOPMENT

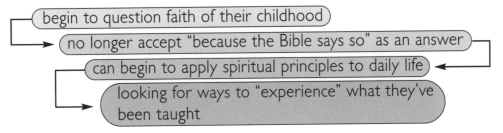

- begin to question faith of their childhood
- no longer accept "because the Bible says so" as an answer
- can begin to apply spiritual principles to daily life
- looking for ways to "experience" what they've been taught

I want you to drift back to your junior high years again. (Don't put the book down because you'll probably need to glance at it a few times.) Take another look at each of the developmental areas listed above and put yourself back in your junior high shoes. This time around may be a little more uncomfortable.

How was it? Did some memories pop into your head? They did for me. Actually, it's a little bit like going to the dentist—I don't like the process, but it's always beneficial.

The bottom line is simply this: The more you understand about the world today's junior high students live in, and the more you are willing to remember about yourself at that age, the more effective you will be as a youth worker. I know a lot of insecure, selfish, easily influenced, but well-intentioned junior highers. I also know that I used to be one.

IDEAS TO STAY IN TOUCH WITH *THE* JUNIOR HIGH WORLD

Watch MTV once in a while.

Read the magazines your students are reading.

Stroll through a local mall and window-shop at stores aimed at teens.

Volunteer at lunchtime at a local junior high.

Spend 15 minutes a day surfing the Internet.

IDEAS TO STAY IN TOUCH WITH *YOUR* JUNIOR HIGH WORLD

If you still have them, check out your old junior high yearbooks.

Drive through your old neighborhood.

Walk the halls of your junior high school.

Dig through your box of old trophies and awards.

Ask your parents to share their memories of your junior high years.

I talk to dozens and dozens of junior high workers each month. My experience has been that typically those who are struggling or frustrated in their ministry have failed to recognize and appreciate the uniqueness of the age they work with. Instead of embracing and valuing the changes junior high students are going through, they are often frustrated by them. As adults, they have forgotten what it's like to be in junior high.

However, most of the junior high youth workers I know are having the time of their lives! They not only love junior highers, they actually *like* them! They understand the changes this age group is facing and they enjoy the unique challenges presented.

LISTEN UP!

"I like being in junior high because it means I'm starting to grow up."
—Steve, seventh grade

Chances are most of you reading this book find yourself in the second category. You are serving right where you belong. You are having fun and your ministry is bearing fruit. Others of you find yourself in the first category—you like the idea of junior high ministry, but find yourself frustrated. In that case I hope this chapter has encouraged you. A few of you may even be in junior high ministry for the wrong reason. Maybe the youth pastor asked for your help and in a moment of weakness you said yes. Perhaps you've made it your life mission to "straighten out this generation." You may love junior highers because you're a Christian, but can't think of a reason to like them. If this is you, there are two choices. You can quit reading now and return your book (since this is only chapter one, it should still look new), or you can prayerfully read on. Be warned however, that the more you read, the more you will fall in "like" with junior highers.

I hope you'll take that chance!

CHEW ON THIS

one What are some issues facing today's junior highers that you didn't face?

two Use five words to describe yourself as a junior higher.

three Can you name of any of the bands, songs, movies or TV shows that your students like?

four On the next page, list three things you plan to do in an attempt to stay current on the world of today's junior high student.

five On a scale of 1 to 10, how well do you "like" junior highers?

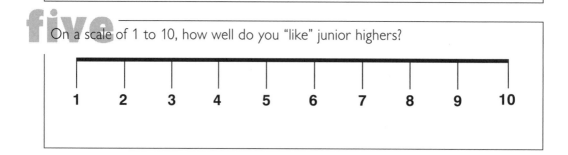

1   2   3   4   5   6   7   8   9   10

CHAOTIC THOUGHTS

CHAPTER TWO

PEOPLE WHO WANT TO HELP

I don't use the word "hero" very often. I tend to think that word should be reserved for people who have saved children from burning buildings or lost limbs fighting for our country. My friend Rick

"I like it when adults are silly and know how to have fun."
—Michael, seventh grade

Williams has done neither of these, but I'd still call him a hero. Rick's name has never appeared on the front-page headlines. Barbara Walters has never offered to interview him on prime-time television, but she should. Rick is a hero because he has spent almost twenty years volunteering in the junior high ministry of his church. Let me say that again . . . twenty years as a junior high volunteer! Rick's not only a hero, he deserves a medal for bravery!

I've had the privilege of being in full-time junior high ministry since 1988. One of the benefits of being in it long-term is that I get the opportunity to talk to a lot of other junior high youth workers. The subject brought up more than any other is volunteers. How can I find more of the right kind? What qualities should I look for in a volunteer? What kind of process should they go through?

What roles should they play? This chapter is designed to help you in your effort to develop effective volunteers for your junior high ministry. You may not believe this, but there are other Rick Williamses out there—we've just got to find them!

WHY DO I NEED HELP?

Yes, this is still a question I hear once in a while. Usually it's from people who have junior high groups that are smaller in size. If you have a smaller ministry, it's easy to feel like you can carry the load alone. While it may be possible to fly solo in your ministry to junior high students, it's not wise. Alone, your ministry is limited. When others join the effort, ministry begins to multiply.

Multiple personalities

While one youth worker with multiple personalities would be interesting, I think it's more effective to have multiple youth workers that each have only one personality! I'm not saying that there is only one personality that makes for an effective junior high volunteer, but I do believe the more people you have involved in leading your students, the more variety your students will experience. Not every student is attracted to the outgoing, verbally expressive leader, so having a volunteer who is more soft-spoken multiplies your ministry. Some of your students are intellectuals, so having a leader who thinks deep thoughts multiplies your ministry.

I'm a loud, high-energy, up-front kind of leader. My wife is a quiet, behind-the-scenes leader. I like to say hi for two seconds to every student that walks through our doors and then move on. My wife tends to pinpoint one student and spend 10-15 minutes hearing about her day. I call everyone "dude." My wife learns everyone's name. My wife and I have very different personalities, but we're both very effective junior high youth workers. In fact, it's our differences that make us effective as a team. Your junior high ministry is made up of students with a variety of personalities. Your adult leadership team should be varied as well.

Multiple gifts

This may shock you, but you are not the world's most gifted person. Even if you are, you don't have an unlimited amount of talent and ability. Because you are limited, you need others on your team to pick up some of the slack. Romans 12:5, 6 says,

". . . We are all parts of his [Christ's] one body, and each of us has different work to do. And since we are all one body in Christ, we belong to each other, and each of us needs all the others. God has given each of us the ability to do certain things well. . . ." (NLT).

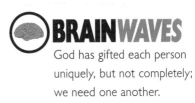

God has gifted each person uniquely, but not completely; we need one another.

I believe God has gifted each person uniquely, but not completely; we need one another. If the junior high ministry I lead only benefited from what I'm good at, they wouldn't benefit much! Instead, we have a team of adults who, together, are gifted in some incredible ways. Our team is made up of moms, dads, college-age students and even a few older high school students. It takes each of us using our individual strengths to multiply our ministry and make it effective.

Multiple resources

I have limited resources and so do you. By resources I mean things like time, money and other "stuff." I have only so much time, money and stuff to pour into junior high ministry. When multiple adults are involved in your ministry, guess what? You immediately multiply the amounts of time, money and stuff available at your disposal.

BRAINWAVES
Ministry is meant to be shared.

As you can see, there are many reasons why it's important to bring others alongside you as you minister. Ministry is meant to be shared. If you are feeling fulfilled in your role as a junior high youth worker, share it with someone else. Let him or her in on the joy! If you are feeling unfulfilled, it could be because you are carrying too much of the load yourself.

WHAT DO I LOOK FOR IN A VOLUNTEER?

I have just spent a fair amount of time convincing you of something you probably already knew: you need others to help your ministry succeed. Most youth workers are already aware they need help. In fact, most youth workers want lots of help right away!

Because we're often desperate for help, men and women who lead youth ministries often take anyone who is breathing and willing to help out. Actually, as long as they're breathing, we'll take 'em—we tend to worry about the willing part later.

I learned a lesson early on in my ministry career. When it comes to volunteers, quality is better than quantity. Having fewer of the right type of junior high leaders is always better than having more of the wrong type. If you aren't asking these questions, let me ask them for you: "What do I look for in a junior high volunteer? What type is the right type?"

In our ministry, we've compiled a list of seven key qualities we look for in a potential junior high volunteer.

ONE SPIRITUAL MATURITY

Because of the unique nature of junior high ministry, we look for volunteers who have strong character and are willing and able to answer the tough questions that junior highers are beginning to ask. Unfortunately, many churches think the junior high department is the perfect place for the young, immature leader to "cut his teeth."

TWO SOWER MENTALITY

We're looking for people who understand the fact that youth ministry is a process, and that we won't always see immediate results. The world is full of Christians who were exposed to the gospel in junior high, but didn't become believers until later.

THREE FUN

We're looking for adults who don't take themselves too seriously. We want leaders who can laugh at themselves and see the fun in everyday living.

BRAINWAVES

When it comes to volunteers, quality is always better than quantity.

FOUR CONTAGIOUS

There needs to be something about each leader that attracts students.

 **PATIENT**

Short-tempered, easily frustrated leaders do more harm than good.

 **AFFIRMING**

We live in a world of put-downs and sarcasm. Junior high students desperately need to feel affirmed, loved and accepted.

SEVEN **LIKES JUNIOR HIGHERS**

We're looking for volunteers who don't just love junior highers—they actually like 'em!

BRAINWAVES
Forget stereotypes!
Take another look at the list. I don't think you'll find any of the "stereotypes" that many people feel are necessary to be an effective junior high worker. Let me give you a quick list of some of the stereotypes people have of an effective junior high worker:

STEREOTYPES OF AN EFFECTIVE JUNIOR HIGH VOLUNTEER

YOUNG	ATHLETIC	LIKES TO WRESTLE
GOOD-LOOKING	TAN	LIKES TO WRESTLE
PLAYS GUITAR	OWNS A VAN	HAS TONS OF
FREE TIME AND LIKES TO SPEND IT WRESTLING		

If this is what it takes to be a junior high youth worker, most of us won't cut it! When I compare myself to these stereotypes, I get more than a little discouraged. Here's where I find hope: Junior high students don't need another cool, young friend. What they *do* need is spiritually-mature adults who love God, who like junior highers and want to be part of their lives.

There are two primary reasons junior high ministries end up with the wrong leaders:

1. Many junior high ministries really don't know what they're looking for in a volunteer. That's why we have our list. We use it as a filter for potential volunteers to help us build a healthy team.

2. We're often desperate and take any and all comers. I know you need help, but you don't need help so badly that you can afford to let the wrong people have influence in your ministry to young teens.

WHAT'S THE PROCESS?

How can you guarantee that the people you plug into your junior high ministry team are going to be the right people? You can't. You can, however, help your chances by putting a process in place that helps guide you as you talk to potential volunteers.

LISTEN UP!

"One piece of advice I would give adults . . . calm down, we're going to turn out okay."
—Erin, eighth grade

You need a process that provides some simple steps that will allow every potential volunteer to get to know your ministry and you to get to know him. Here's an example:

POTENTIAL VOLUNTEER
attends church membership class

POTENTIAL VOLUNTEER
expresses interest in junior high ministry

POTENTIAL VOLUNTEER receives junior high ministry information, purpose statement, application and reference letters

POTENTIAL VOLUNTEER observes junior high program

POTENTIAL VOLUNTEER meets with junior high director for interview after receiving reference letters and background check/fingerprinting

POTENTIAL VOLUNTEER begins ministry in junior high department or is directed toward another ministry that he is spiritually shaped for

 **BRAIN WAVES**

A "process" doesn't guarantee you'll find the right volunteers, but it sure helps!

Our ministry uses a ten-step process to implement adult volunteers. The list above is simply a sample that shows what I think are the most important pieces of our process.

Here are a few reasons why having a process is important:

SERVES It serves as a source of protection for you and your ministry.

ATTRACTS It attracts quality leaders.

GIVES It gives both you and the potential volunteer a platform to ask questions.

DETERS It deters those who have improper motives.

MAKES It makes your ministry appear more professional and credible.

GAINS It gains trust in the eyes of your church leadership and parents.

In effect, the process becomes one great big application. A written application alone doesn't give you insight into how the potential volunteer interacts with students. On the flip side, the ability to be fun and interact well with students isn't in itself a good enough reason to give someone a leadership role in your ministry. No single step in the process is adequate on its own, but when combined with the other steps, the total picture helps you in your effort to recruit the best possible leaders for your students.

I realize that many of you may be thinking something like, "Jeepers, with that strict a process, he's lucky to get any help at all!" Or, "Golly, it sure seems like it's hard to become a volunteer in that ministry!" Words like "jeepers" and "golly" may not be in your vocabulary, but I grew up watching Gomer Pyle reruns.

BRAINWAVES

Make it hard for volunteers to get into your ministry, but easy to get out.

I believe in the "Hard to get in, easy to get out" philosophy of youth ministry. I make it hard on a volunteer to get into our ministry because I want to ensure quality leadership. I make it easy for a volunteer to get out by not asking him to sign a one-year contract or agree to six months of ministry or anything like that. If someone wants to move on, it doesn't do that person or our junior high ministry any good to keep him on board simply to fulfill a commitment he made that he now regrets.

WHAT ROLES CAN VOLUNTEERS PLAY?

Since most junior high ministries are entirely volunteer-led, it's obvious that volunteers can play any and every role necessary to help make your church's junior high ministry effective. I think two good questions to ask a volunteer are these:

1. What are you gifted at?
2. How can you use that gift in our ministry?

We have volunteers who lead small groups, teach on weekends, organize events, oversee other volunteers, lead ministry teams, organize parent events, cook, send care packages to sick students, write follow-up letters and encourage new believers. You name it, our volunteers do it!

Let me point back to the process for a minute. The process allows me, as the point person of our ministry, to get to know the personality, gifts, weaknesses and ministry goals of a potential volunteer before he or she is ever placed into ministry. This helps volunteers jump right into a role that fits them best and will bear the most fruit in their lives and in the lives of students.

IF I'M THE POINT PERSON, WHAT'S MY ROLE?

Your role as the point person is threefold. First, you chart the course and lead the way. Second, you represent the interests and concerns of the ministry to the rest of the church (including the person you answer to, elders and parents). Third, you provide TLC to the rest of the volunteers on your team. TLC is my interpretation of Ephesians 4:11, 12:

"It was he who gave some to be apostles, some to be prophets, some to be evangelists, and some to be pastors and teachers, to prepare God's people for works of service, so that the body of Christ may be built up."

BRAINWAVES
The role of the point person is to provide training, leadership and care to the rest of the team.

If you are the point person for your junior high ministry, your role is to prepare people for works of service. I do this through what I call "Volunteer TLC."

TRAINING

Some of the ways you can do this include providing monthly training meetings, forwarding copies of helpful articles, supplying books (personally, I think you should provide two copies of this book to every volunteer in your ministry—just in case they lose one) and providing opportunities to attend seminars and conferences.

LISTEN UP!

"I don't like it when adults try to prove their point by saying, 'When I was your age . . .'"
—Kendra, seventh grade

LEADERSHIP

Your job is to chart the course, lead the way, take the heat, pass the credit, do whatever you can to pave the way for success.

CARE

Carry this out by having one-on-one lunches, sending birthday cards, notes of encouragement, sending e-mails and through prayer support.

Questions: Doesn't the point person have to teach? No. The point person simply has to ensure the quality of the teaching. Doesn't the point person have to handle all the money? No. The point person just needs to make sure the money is being handled properly. Doesn't the point person have to . . . NO! The point person needs to provide training, leadership and care to the rest of the team so they are empowered to minister.

I know what you're thinking. "Man, that sure leaves a lot of free time for the youth pastor to golf while volunteers are doing all the work." Look, I've seen a lot of youth pastors golf, and it's obvious that, as a whole, they aren't spending much time honing their skills.

My friend Rick Williams has never saved a child from a burning building or been injured in war. He is, however, a junior high ministry volunteer and that makes him and those of you like him a true hero.

CHEW ON THIS

one
On a piece of paper, make a list of the volunteers in your junior high ministry. Now go down the list and write two or three words to describe each one's personality. For example: Outgoing, fun, but serious.

two
Do you have a "multiple personality" group of volunteers?

three
Take another look at my seven key qualities of a junior high volunteer. What are some other characteristics you look for in a volunteer?

four
Do you have a structured process for identifying and implementing potential volunteers? If it isn't satisfactory, jot down some ideas to make it more effective.

five What roles are you fulfilling that you can share with others?

six On a scale of 1 to 10, how well do you provide training, leadership and care to your volunteer team?

```
 1    2    3    4    5    6    7    8    9    10
```

CHAOTIC THOUGHTS

"If parents are for you, who can be against you?" —Katie Edwards

CHAPTER THREE

PARENTS

The summer sun was blazing, we were running late and the church bus was crammed full with junior highers. Just as I turned the key to start the engine, a frantic dad pounded on the bus door. He had noticed how full the bus was and wouldn't let me pull away until he had personally walked through the bus to make sure every student had a seat. My initial thought was "What an idiot!" I quickly felt convicted for my attitude and changed my thought to "What a dork!"

Two minutes later, the inspection was over and the dad filled me in on his findings. "Kurt, there is a seat for every student, and you actually have room for two more riders." I wanted to respond in the junior high vernacular of the time . . . "Duh!" Instead I thanked him for his concern and headed the bus toward the freeway.

Now that I have children of my own, I see things in a whole new light. The first time my daughter gets on a bus for a day at the beach, guess what I'll do? I'll not only make sure she has a safe

BRAINWAVES

Three Keys to Parents:
1. Earn their trust.
2. Earn their trust.
3. Earn their trust.

seat, but I'll also stare down a few eighth grade guys who may actually be thinking about talking to the cute new seventh grade girl . . . *my* girl.

Parents . . . they're everywhere! Think about this: There are at least twice as many parents in your junior high ministry as there are students. They come in a variety of forms: biological parents, stepparents, single parents, grandparents, adopted parents, aunts, uncles and older siblings, just to name a few. Every student in your ministry is being raised by someone, and that someone usually loves his or her young teen very much.

In many churches in America, junior high ministry is under the youth ministry umbrella that includes junior high, senior high and college-age students. Because of the nature of twelve- to fourteen-year-olds, I think this is appropriate. Junior high students have more in common with high schoolers than with children in elementary school. There is, however, one area in which junior high ministry has much in common with children's ministry—parents.

There can be no children's ministry without the support and trust of parents. Third graders still rely on mom and dad to drive them to church, to pick them up after an event and to fork over their hard-earned dollars to pay for the variety of activities the church offers. The same is true with junior high students.

At the high school level, parents can basically say things like, "Hey, we don't really like that you go to church, but here are the car keys to drive yourself there." Or, "Now that you have a job, you can spend your money how you like. If you want to spend your money on church activities, feel free to do so." It's important for high school ministries to earn the trust and support of parents, but because of the increasing independence of high school students, it isn't quite as critical.

For your ministry to junior high students to be successful, however, it is crucial that parents support and trust your efforts to minister to their children. In this chapter, we'll take a look at why parents are so important, how to gain their trust and how you can utilize them to your advantage in your ministry.

WHY PARENTS ARE IMPORTANT

Parents are entrusting you with their most precious possession.

The vast majority of parents try hard. Granted, none of them are perfect, and as youth workers, we often hear about their shortcomings from their disgruntled teenagers. Flawed as the parents of your students may be, there is usually one common denominator: they love their kids and want what's best for them. The wise junior high leader understands the love parents have for their children and that this love often results in crazy requests . . . like wanting to know a few details about the weeklong trip to Iraq that your ministry is planning.

LISTEN UP!

"My dad lets me go to church because at least I'm not playing tag on the freeway."
—Bryan, eighth grade

Instead of being bothered by the barrage of questions you receive every time you plan an activity, put yourself in the shoes of a parent. If you aren't already, chances are that someday you, too, will be the mom or dad of a junior higher. Then you'll probably find yourself saying, "Now I see!"

Parents talk to one another.

They talk a lot. They talk about soccer, about school, about the neighborhood kids and yes, they talk a lot about your junior high ministry. They talk about things they know, things they don't know, things they think they know and things they *think* they *should* know. I'm a parent, and I talk . . . a lot!

Parents have influence.

I don't know how big your junior high ministry is, but I do know that despite its size, there are influential parents represented. Elders and deacons, Sunday school teachers, church employees, pastors, committee members and the like are all influential decision makers in your church, and chances are you are ministering to some of their children. Parents also have influence simply because they make up a large percentage of your church's attendance and are responsible for a large percentage of your church's income. This sounds a lot like church politics because it is church politics. Instead of running from it, or pretending it doesn't exist, my advice is to use it to your advantage.

Parents have stuff you need.

Not only do you need parents' trust, you need their things! You need their homes. You need their swimming pools, Suburbans and satellite dishes. You need their minivans, megaphones and microwaves. You need their tents, tackle boxes and tables. You need their wit, wisdom and willingness. Unless Bill Gates is cutting monthly checks to your junior high ministry, you can't afford everything you need. Parents have almost everything you need and are amazingly willing to let a *trusted* adult use it.

Parents dictate your effectiveness.

You may be the coolest, best-looking, most athletic junior high worker on the planet. You may know how to drop into a half-pipe without breaking your neck. You may be full of wisdom, experience and patience. You may even remember a few Greek and

Hebrew words from seminary. But it really doesn't matter who you are or what you can do. As a seasoned junior high youth worker, I can tell you that effective junior high ministry boils down to two things: The sovereignty of God and the support of parents.

HOW TO EARN THEIR TRUST

In no particular order, here are a few ideas to help you and your ministry earn the much-needed trust of parents.

Communicate regularly.

Junior high parents want, need and deserve to know what's going on. Don't rely on your students to get information to their parents. Instead, communicate to students' parents regularly about upcoming events, activities, needs and prayer requests. Because parents are busy, the best approach is to give them information that they can access when it's convenient for them to do so. E-mails, monthly newsletters and updated websites are effective, nonintrusive ways to keep parents informed. An informed parent is usually a happy parent.

Don't make unnecessary changes.

Parents are grown-ups, and grown-ups don't like change. Avoid making changes that may seem small to you but are, in reality, big to parents. Costs of events, time and place of meetings and registration deadlines may seem like insignificant changes to you, but can be a real source of frustration to parents.

BRAINWAVES
Trust is earned in the little things.

Proofread all written material.

I believe that trust is earned in the little things. Typos, wrong addresses and poor grammar on printed material can really harm your efforts. In the workforce world of parents, such mistakes aren't tolerated. Parents aren't going to be real excited about investing several hundred dollars to send their child to "Sumar Cump." You've probably heard stories of church bulletin "bloopers." Don't just rely on "spell check" on your computer. If you don't feel qualified to perform the necessary proofreading, look for someone in your ministry who is uniquely gifted for that task.

Work with them, not against them.

Raising teenagers is no easy task, and many of your parents are doing it for the first time. By allowing you to influence their child's life, they are putting a ton of trust in you. Be sure that the language and conversations in your ministry support the authority and honor of parents. Talk with parents and ask them what you can do to help support their efforts. If a parent thinks you are purposely undermining him or her, you have lost trust and, most likely, a student's presence in your ministry.

Don't abuse their generosity.

Earlier, I mentioned that parents have stuff you need. When you are fortunate enough to get the keys to the minivan, be sure to say

"My parents think our junior high group is cool . . . they always ask me if they can come too."

—Derek, seventh grade

thanks. In fact, don't just say thanks, but say thanks and keep it clean. Actually, say thanks, keep it clean and return it with a full tank of gas. Better yet, say thanks, keep it clean, return it with a full tank of gas and don't ask to use it again for a while.

Minimize mistakes.

Nobody's perfect, and parents understand this. They understand no ministry is perfect, that accidents happen and that things sometimes go wrong. The key word is *sometimes*. If your ministry is marked by imperfection, accidents and mistakes, they'll begin to lose trust in you and the ministry you're leading.

Act your age.

Ouch! This one hurts a little. As youth workers, we are in a quandary. We are adults, but we spend much of our lives

Be willing to admit when you're wrong.

with teenagers. I'm convinced that youth workers make up a huge percentage of the adults who still buy surfboard-, skateboard- and snowboard-related clothing. Certainly no other group of adults watches as much MTV as we do. I'd even be willing to bet that many of your homes and garages are filled with video games, skateboards and Super Soakers. Mine certainly is.

This is all well and good, but be certain that in your efforts to relate to students you don't distance yourself from parents. Parents find it hard to trust a 30-year-old who shows up at church with ultra-baggy shorts, spiked hair, a nose ring and a tattoo on his arm . . . even if it is a cool picture of Jesus!

Create an "open door."

Invite parents to pop in on your meetings unannounced. Let them see your ministry in action. Our parents know that they are always welcome to drop by and see our ministry for themselves. Most of them never take advantage of the opportunity, but knowing they have that freedom is reassuring.

Stick around awhile.

Longevity is the single most effective method of earning the trust of parents. Earning trust takes time. Parents want to see proof in the pudding. Don't expect parents to trust you simply because you have an education and a smile. Don't expect them to blindly hand their students to you solely on the basis of your position. Parents will trust you when they know you've been around awhile and that you plan on staying. Since the average tenure of a youth worker is less than eighteen months, someone who sticks around

a few years will enjoy the trust of parents . . . even if you happen to have a tattoo of Jesus on your arm.

TOP 10 THINGS *NOT* TO SAY TO PARENTS

10. "Don't worry about it."

9. "What's the big deal?"

8. "I'm sure if we left your daughter at camp there was a good reason."

7. "About the minivan we borrowed . . ."

6. "And you think that's my fault?"

5. "I know you're disappointed, but he's only copying the behavior modeled at home."

4. "If I were you . . ."

3. "Look, if you would spend a little more time with your child . . ."

2. "Calm down."

1. "Trust me."

HOW TO UTILIZE PARENTS IN YOUR MINISTRY

Parents are important, and it's important to earn their trust. But beyond that, are they really of any value to your junior high ministry? Of course they are. It's good to know that parents are important. It's important to know that you need their trust. However, it's incredibly advantageous to understand that they can also play vital roles in your ministry to their children. Here are just a few roles parents can play in your church's junior high ministry. I've put these into three categories: roles of the heart, the head and the hands.

The heart

Some parents have a unique love for junior highers. Granted, every parent loves their own kid, but some of them actually like other junior highers too! These are the parents you want as members of your volunteer team. Many youth workers make the mistake of sidelining parents. Often this is because they don't trust their motives, or they've heard horror stories of controlling parents trying to force their agendas onto the ministry.

I believe that another reason for lack of parental involvement is due to insecure leaders. An insecure leader doesn't want older, wiser adults around to raise the bar. A secure leader understands the value of surrounding himself with partners in ministry who are farther down life's road. The parents of your students will value and trust your ministry a little more when they know there are other parents who are playing a vital role.

Obviously, not every parent who wants to volunteer in your ministry should be allowed to do so, but a wise youth worker understands that someone with a heart for junior highers is a valuable commodity, even if he happens to be a parent.

The head

Have you ever had a parent say to you, "Hey, I was thinking about you yesterday"? Or, "Every day when I pick my daughter up from school, I'm reminded about the importance of your ministry"? Or, "I thought of something the other day that you might be interested in"?

"How come we can't bug our parents, but they're allowed to bug us?"
—Jared, seventh grade

I absolutely love these kinds of parents! Why? Because they're thinking about me and our ministry to their children. Better yet, their thoughts are of a positive nature! How, exactly, can you involve these parents in your ministry?

Here are some practical suggestions:

 Ask these parents to pray for your ministry. Since they seem to think about your ministry a lot, why not ask them to pray for it too?

Give these parents your e-mail address and invite their input, suggestions and concerns. They might give you something to think about that you hadn't considered or head off a potential problem at the pass.

 Ask these parents to be your public "cheerleaders"—to wave the banner of your junior high ministry wherever they can.

"Pick their brain" every once in a while. Ask for their parental viewpoint. Invite them to brainstorm a situation with you.

Parents are your allies, not your enemies.

These parents aren't necessarily ready or even qualified to join your volunteer team, but you and your ministry seem to be on their mind regularly—and as they say, "A mind is a terrible thing to waste."

The hands

Most of your parents have two hands. Some are very talented with them. Others may not be so talented, but are willing to "lend them out" when needed.

There isn't a junior high worker in the world who doesn't need the help of willing parents from time to time. Parents willing to help build stuff, paint stuff, move stuff, fix stuff, pick stuff up and drop stuff off.

"Let me know if you ever need a hand." These words are music to the desperate junior high worker's ears. When a parent says this to you, be sure to make a note of it and put it in a safe place. If necessary, get their name and phone number tattooed on your arm just below the picture of Jesus.

Again, these parents may not be the type you want as regular volunteers. Heck, they may not even think about you all that often. What they do have is a pair of hands that they seem willing to use. And as they say, "A pair of hands is a terrible thing to waste"—or something like that.

Parents . . . they're everywhere! Too many junior high workers view them as the enemy. Instead, view them as allies. Understand their importance, earn their trust and utilize them in your ministry. I think you'll be glad you did.

CHEW ON THIS

one Make a list of the five most influential parents in your ministry.

two Create another list of parents in your ministry who have resources you need. Write down what those resources are and how they can impact your ministry.

three Write down the words "heart," "head" and "hands." Under each one, list the names of parents who fall into each category.

four

Compile a list of the parents who trust you the most. Then list those whose trust you still need to earn.

five

Take another look at the various lists you've created. On a scale of 1 to 10, how well do you think you know the parents of your students?

1	2	3	4	5	6	7	8	9	10

CHAOTIC THOUGHTS

"Intelligent people are always open to new ideas. In fact, they look for them." —Proverbs 18:15, NLT

CHAPTER FOUR

PRACTICING CREATIVITY

Guess what? You can be creative. Yes, you! Right away many of you thought something like this: "Uh, no I can't, and I don't think I want to read this chapter." Yes you can, and yes you do.

No other ministry in the church feels the pressure to be creative quite as much as we do. Do any of these thoughts sound familiar?

"We need to find a new game for Wednesday night."

"Let's write a skit to go with our lesson."

"We need to make a funny video for Sunday."

"We need fresher graphics on our website."

"How can we liven up our talks?"

While these thoughts may not occur frequently in other areas of ministry, in junior high ministry they happen over lunch. Because of the nature of what we do, the ability to think outside the box seems like a prerequisite for success.

Here, in the box, is a short list of additional areas that tirelessly stretch our creativity.

THINGS THAT SCREAM FOR CREATIVITY

CAMP THEMES   LESSON TOPICS   GAMES
PUBLICITY FLYERS   DECORATIONS   HUMOR
PRIZES   VIDEOS   DRAMA   DISCIPLINE
INCREASING ATTENDANCE   ACTIVITIES
CROWDBREAKERS   SMALL GROUP DISCUSSIONS
DISCIPLESHIP   PROBLEM-SOLVING

I cut that list a little short because, frankly, I was starting to get a stomachache thinking about all the stuff in my junior-high-youth-worker world that pressures me to be creative. I'll bet your world isn't much different from mine. Junior high workers feel a need to provide a ministry that is fresh, current, relevant, real and cutting-edge.

This pressure comes from a variety of sources. It can come from parents who compare our ministry to the junior high program at their old church. It can come from pastors who compare our ministry to the church down the street. It can come from those who compare our ministry to what it used to look like. It can come from students who live in a world that spends billions of dollars to catch their attention. It can come from our pride. It can come from our insecurity. It can come from our desire to please. Like I said, I feel constant pressure to be creative. Unfortunately, most of that pressure comes from unhealthy sources.

BRAINWAVES
Creativity is not an option.

Creativity is in the same camp as money, sex, power, fame and prestige. These things alone aren't bad; it's the motive behind them that can cause problems. Even though some of the pressure I feel to be creative comes from unhealthy motives, I know that, for the most part, I'm driven by what I like to call "creative integrity." Creative integrity occurs when I'm motivated by the following factors:

CREATIVE INTEGRITY

I want to do all things as unto the Lord. HE DESERVES MY BEST EFFORT.

It's a privilege to minister to junior high students. THEY DESERVE MY BEST EFFORT.

The church has entrusted me. IT DESERVES MY BEST EFFORT.

It is a privilege to present the gospel. THIS DESERVES MY BEST EFFORT.

GIVING MY BEST EFFORT demands creativity.

The world does an incredible job of convincing us of its second-rate messages. Unfortunately, the church often does a second-rate job of convincing the world of its incredible message. Creative integrity drives me to do the best I can to reach junior high students with the message of Christ. There's no avoiding it. Creativity is in your job description. Giving your best to God, your students and your church demands it.

Before we talk about how to strengthen your creative confidence, let me give you my working definition of creativity. In junior high ministry, creativity can be defined as "the willingness to try something in a new and improved way." That takes some of the pressure off, doesn't it! Creativity isn't the ability to create something incredible out of nothing—it's the willingness to take what you have and make it better than you have in the past. That's it! It means that instead of going to the file cabinet and pulling out last

You *are* creative!

year's lesson on forgiveness, you go to the file cabinet, pull out last year's lesson on forgiveness and improve it!

I'm not a creative guy in the traditional sense. I've never invented anything. I haven't had too many people gasp in amazement at my new idea or creative solution. I am, however, willing to try new things and look for a better way to do the stuff I'm already doing. I hope you are too.

PROOF THAT YOU ARE CREATIVE

You are creative, and I can prove it!

You have a relationship with the Creator.

God spoke the world into existence. He created life. He is the author of all that science has discovered and all that science is yet to figure out. He is the Creator of everything known and unknown, and guess what? He calls you by name. He not only calls you by name, he calls you his child. Now's a good time to pause and let that soak in for a minute. Actually, why don't you read this paragraph one more time?

As God's child, you're probably accustomed to asking for his provision. You ask God for safety, peace, wisdom, comfort, forgiveness and more. You recognize that everything that is good in your life is because of his love for you.

I'm not sure how you came to the conclusion that you wanted to work with junior high students, but I hope it included some prayer and a sense that this is where God wants you to impact his kingdom. If this is where God wants you, he will give you the tools and gifts you need in order to fulfill his calling. You can be creative because you are a child of the Creator!

You are creative when you want to be.

I don't like taking out the trash. I never have and I never will. Since childhood, this weekly ritual has been a thorn in my flesh. When I was in junior high, I came up with what I thought was a creative approach to my dilemma. I figured it would be much easier to empty the trash in the house once a month rather than once a week. I could achieve this by simply stomping in each trash can and, in essence, become my very own human trash compactor. When I told my parents about this idea, they decided to let me give it a try. (Can you believe it?)

The following month, instead of taking the household trash outside, I made my rounds from room to room compressing the trash with my foot. It worked beautifully . . . that is, until the day came for me to empty each wastebasket. I knew I was in trouble when I went to pick up the trash can from the bathroom. It seemed to weigh about 25 pounds. Not only was it heavy, but I discovered that the trash didn't dump out as easily as it had in the past. I had to literally dig the dirty, slimy bathroom trash out of its home with my hands. It had been a wonderful month of stomping, pressing and crushing trash, but the next 15 minutes was spent pulling trash out of overstuffed containers.

Even though I don't think I'm a creative guy by nature, this story

BRAINWAVES
Everyone's creative when they're in a pinch.

reminds me that I can come up with some creative ideas (I said *creative*, not *good*) when I want to. To this day, I still wrestle with the weekly chore of taking out the trash, and to this day I'm still creatively trying to get out of it.

What's the last thing you wanted really badly? A nice vacation? Some new flooring for your home? To be noticed by that certain someone? To replace that worn-out furniture? That new outfit that was just a little out of your price range? I'm not sure what it was, but I am sure you figured out a creative way to get it. My wife will tell you that I'm fairly adept at creatively figuring out ways to get what I want.

Sadly, I'm also creative at coming up with excuses. Failing to complete a project on time. An unfinished task around the house. Forgetting to pick up my daughter from school. These types of

LISTENUP!
"I think the games we play are weird. They're fun, but really weird."
—Haley, seventh grade

things have resulted in a sudden burst of creativity more than once in my life. I imagine they have for you too.

I know you can be creative . . . if you want to be.

You used to be five years old.

At one time in your life you were five. It's hard to find an unimaginative, uncreative five-year-old. Just for fun, take a walk through the five-year-old class at your church. Spend a few minutes watching and listening. You'll see kids driving invisible cars, eating invisible food and talking to invisible friends. You'll hear girls telling incredible stories to go along with their simple drawings. You'll find boys using cars, blocks, shoes, anything at all as guns. Why they do this, I don't know. I just know that they do.

I think five-year-old children are the world's most creative human beings—and you used to be one of them!

A while back, I walked into my backyard to find my five-year-old daughter, Kayla, playing with a few of her friends. They had somehow managed to remove the roof from her playhouse. They had turned the roof upside down and were using it as a canoe. For paddles, they were using the plastic supports that had, only moments earlier, held the roof in place. Kayla quickly warned me not to step onto the grass because it was, in her words, "really red-hot lava." When I asked her why the plastic oars weren't melting in the really red-hot lava she said, "Because we went to Target and bought some lava protector stuff for them."

After they had finished playing, I spent the next 30 minutes trying to reassemble a roof that three little girls had dismantled in 30 seconds. As cute, charming and wonderful as Kayla is (after all, she's my daughter), she is not unlike anyone else who is, was or will be five. Five-year-olds are creative.

Something begins to happen as we grow up. It starts as early as second or third grade. The things that gained us praise when we were five now get us into trouble. When we were five, we could be as silly and creative as we wanted to be—in fact, it was encouraged. As we grow older, creativity is no longer encouraged and, all too often, is squelched.

BRAINWAVES

Creativity is an attitude, not an aptitude.

If I walked into the backyard of one of my junior high students and saw him rowing a pretend canoe through a sea of pretend lava, I wouldn't think it was cute; I'd think it was goofy. If my senior pastor walked into my office and found me playing with army

67

men under my desk, he wouldn't think it was creative; he'd think it was cause for a counseling session. As five-year-olds, we were taught to dream and imagine, but as we grew up, we were expected to be realistic and to "act our age." This is a natural process, but I think there is an unfortunate side to it. Many adults forget how to think creatively. They forget that they were once five years old.

You are creative. I know you are because you have a relationship with the Creator, you are creative when you want to be and you used to be five years old. You can argue with me if you want, but it will take some pretty creative persuasion (which would, of course, prove that you are creative!).

It seems, in light of these three pieces of evidence, that creativity is an attitude, not an aptitude. Unfortunately, many adults have had an attitude adjustment and no longer use their creative abilities. Let me give you three reasons why:

THREE CREATIVE EXCUSES

ONE **IT TAKES TOO MUCH EFFORT.**

It's easier to do what we've always done. Why take the time to try something new?

TWO **FEAR OF FAILURE.**

There's no need to take unnecessary risks. Swinging for the fence isn't worth the risk of striking out.

THREE

"IF IT AIN'T BROKE, DON'T FIX IT."

Why mess with something that works?

There they are: the three biggest reasons adults choose not to exercise their creative abilities. At first glance, these seem logical. Why *should* we put in unnecessary effort? Why is the risk worth it? Do we *really* need to fix something that isn't broken? Why? Because creative integrity *is* vital to junior high ministry. Effort must be put in, risks must be taken and things that aren't broken must be fixed because God, our church and our students deserve our best efforts.

"Okay," the previously creatively-impaired junior high youth worker thought to himself. "I know I need to stretch my creative muscles, but where can I go to find some tips to help me?" Guess what? They're right here in this chapter . . . amazing!

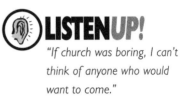

LISTEN UP!

"If church was boring, I can't think of anyone who would want to come."
—Danisha, eighth grade

TIPS FOR CREATIVITY

Plan ahead.

Nothing kills the ability to be creative more than procrastination. Doing something new or even improving something old takes an element of forethought. If you wait until Saturday night to plan your Sunday school lesson, creativity isn't on your mind; survival is. The reason so many youth workers find themselves in the rut of doing the same old stuff is because they don't plan ahead. When we're in a hurry, we always revert back to what is handy.

Find your creative time.

Creative thinking is hard work. Because it takes extra effort, it is wise to do it when you are at your mental peak. If you are a morning person, do your creative work early. If you're a night person, do it late. Don't waste your peak energy on brainless stuff like returning e-mails and cleaning your white board.

Be a looker and a reader.

Take a look at the world around you. There's an old saying that says, "Stop and smell the roses." I say, "Stop, smell the roses and then figure out how to use them in an object lesson." Look around. The world is full of really neat stuff that you can apply to your ministry setting. In addition, be a person who reads. I read everything. Billboards, bus stop ads, restaurant menus, magazines and books. They're full of logos, artwork, ideas and inspiration. In almost everything, there is an object lesson waiting to happen.

Use TV, don't let it use you.

I admit it . . . I'm a television junkie. I've learned, however, to use TV to my advantage. My creative excuse for watching TV is that I might find a really good illustration for my next talk. Hey, it could

All of us are more creative than one of us!

happen! Seriously, the men and women who produce television entertainment are incredibly creative. Don't be afraid to borrow some of their ideas.

Hang around creative people.

There's strength in numbers. Two heads are better than one. Iron sharpens iron. You get my point. One of the best ways to expand your creativity is to spend time with people who seem to ooze it.

Always ask, "Can this be improved?"

Don't settle for the status quo. The second biggest creativity killer

is mediocrity. If you plan ahead, you will
have plenty of time to look at your talk,
evaluate your games, reread your meeting
agenda and ask yourself if it can be improved.

BRAINWAVES

When brainstorming, no
idea is a bad idea.

Empty your mind before beginning.

Instead of reaching for last year's folder, start planning your annu-
al event with an empty pad of paper, asking questions like: "What
if we could hold camp anywhere we wanted?"; "What if money
wasn't an issue?"; "What if . . . What if . . . What if . . . ?" When you
start with an empty mind, you come up with all sorts of ideas.
Most of them will go unused, but a few may stick.

If I asked my wife, "What if you could have any house you wanted?", she'd describe a four-bedroom, country-style house. She'd
want it with a view of the ocean but not too close. Her dream
house would sit on an acre with beautifully-manicured landscap-
ing. She'd also want a wraparound porch, a circular driveway and
a picket fence. Because I earn my living as a junior high pastor, I
can't provide my wife with her dream
house. But because I heard her "what
ifs," I know what I *can* do. I can save my
pennies and buy her that picket fence,
and maybe even give her a picture of the
ocean.

BRAINWAVES

The only time you fail is
when you fail to try something new.

Have an honest ear.

This isn't so much a tip to help you become more creative, as it is
a source of protection for you in the process. You will benefit from
having someone around you who still remains somewhat of a real-
ist. Find someone who is honest enough to tell you when an idea
is a bad one. Give someone permission to question your motives,
to ensure that creative integrity is intact.

Become five again.

Color outside the lines. Dream big dreams. Paddle a canoe through some "really red-hot lava." But be sure to buy some of that lava protector stuff for your oars.

CHEW ON THIS

one Generate a list of those things that scream for your creativity.

two In your setting, what seems to be the most common source of creative pressure?

three Spend five or ten minutes trying to remember what you were like when you were five years old. If necessary, call your parents and ask them to supply you with some memories.

four

Which one of the three creative excuses holds you back most often?

five

On a scale of 1 to 10, how comfortable are you in taking creative risks? Which of the tips for creativity do you need to practice?

```
1    2    3    4    5    6    7    8    9    10
```

CHAOTIC THOUGHTS

CHAPTER FIVE

PLANNING YOUR PROGRAMS

As I sat down to write this chapter, I realized something. This chapter has already been written . . . twice! Almost every principle you will read over the next few pages has already been thoroughly discussed in two books that have had incredible impact in recent years: *The Purpose-Driven Church*, by Rick Warren, and *Purpose-Driven Youth Ministry*, by Doug Fields.

This chapter will provide a brief overview of what a healthy ministry to junior high students looks like, but for an in-depth discussion I suggest you read both *Purpose-Driven* books. The principles in these books apply to any ministry setting, including junior high ministry. I'm often asked if I'm going to write a book on "Purpose-Driven Junior High Ministry." My response is always the same: I don't need to because Doug Fields has already written it. The principles in his book apply to junior high ministry as well as high school ministry.

I'm not going to write a book about it, but I will write a chapter on the subject.

 BRAIN WAVES

The most important question to ask is: "Why does our ministry exist?"

"What" is the most overused word in junior high ministry. That's not a question—it's a statement. Trying to figure out what your junior high ministry is going to do is a topic that most likely takes up a great deal of your time. For example:

"What are we going to do at midweek?"

"What are we going to do for summer activities?"

"What should we do about the rowdy kids that show up?"

"What games should we play this Friday night?"

LISTEN UP!

"God has helped me through some really hard stuff. Actually, I think he's used my small group leader as a way to help me out."
—Amber, seventh grade

These are important questions, but they aren't the questions you should ask first. The first question you need to ask is: "Why does our junior high ministry exist?"

WHY DOES OUR MINISTRY EXIST?

Junior high ministry exists for the same reason all other ministry in the church exists: To fulfill God's biblical purposes. In his book, *The Purpose-Driven Church*, Rick Warren writes about the five biblical purposes God has for your ministry—evangelism, worship, fellowship, discipleship and ministry.

These five purposes are found in two well-known biblical passages, The Great Commandment and The Great Commission (Matthew 22:37-40 and Matthew 28:19, 20). I encourage you to read both Rick's and Doug's books for a detailed discussion on the five biblical purposes. Better yet, crack open your Bible and discover them for yourself!

The second question that should be asked is: "Who is our target?"

WHO IS OUR TARGET?

That's easy. Our target is junior high or middle school students, but there's more to it than that. There are at least five types of junior high students in your area. Instead of simply aiming for junior high students in general, and hoping that one program can reach them all, aim for a specific type of student with a specific program to fulfill a specific biblical purpose. You do want to minister to every student in your community, but how you approach this task will depend on which students you are targeting at the time.

The five types of junior high students in your area are those who could care less about church, those who are curious about church, those who have been caught by Christ, those who are committed to him and finally, those students who are contagious Christians. The words you use to define these students aren't important (in our ministry we use the five words community, crowd, congregation, committed and core). What is important is recognizing that each type of student exists and that each type has its own level of spiritual commitment.

BRAINWAVES

One program can't effectively minister to every student.

TARGET	SPIRITUAL COMMITMENT
Care Less	These students don't attend church—they couldn't care less. They are living apart from Christ.
Curious	These students attend church somewhat regularly—they are curious about the things of God.
Caught	These students have a relationship with Christ and other Christians.
Committed	These students are committed to growing spiritually.
Contagious	These students are actively involved in ministry—they are contagious Christians.

It's important to recognize that as the spiritual commitment increases, the number of students in that particular target audience will decrease, similar to a funnel. There are a lot more junior highers in your community that couldn't care less about church than there are those who are contagious in their faith. Visually, it looks something like this:

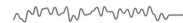

CARE LESS
CURIOUS
CAUGHT
COMMITTED
CONTAGIOUS

That graphic might bother some of you. Shouldn't you try to get every student to show up at every event? NO! A common mistake many youth workers make is to add the phrase "bring a friend" to the end of every announcement. We say things like, "Join us for street witnessing on Friday night . . . and be sure to bring a friend." Or, "We are going to dig deep into God's Word at midweek . . . so be sure to bring a friend." The problem with wanting every student at every program is that not every student is ready for every program. How can a "Care less" junior high student help you street-witness? Leave him on the streets so your contagious students have someone to witness to!

It's perfectly fine to say to students, "This program may not be right for you yet, but let me tell you about one that is." The neat thing about identifying the students in your area is that it not only helps you identify where they are now, but it pro-

LISTEN UP!

"Our church does stuff. We don't just sit around like a bunch of sticks in the mud."
—Greg, eighth grade

vides a goal of where you hope to take them. It also determines what programs can best meet their needs.

Now that you know the five biblical purposes of the church, and have identified the potential targets, you are ready to ask, "How are we going to fulfill the five purposes *and* reach our targets?"

HOW DO WE DO THIS?

In our student ministry, we use a simple formula that helps in our programming efforts. It looks like this:

Potential target + biblical purpose = program

For example, "Care less" students + purpose of evangelism = Harvest Party outreach. Or, "Caught" students + purpose of fellowship = midweek small groups.

We've determined that the best target audience for the purpose of evangelism is those students who couldn't care less about God. Each October we provide an outreach with the hope of making these students a little more curious about God and the church.

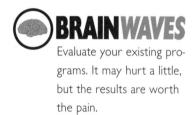

BRAINWAVES

Evaluate your existing programs. It may hurt a little, but the results are worth the pain.

That's what we call strategic junior high ministry! Does this mean everything becomes easy now? Of course not! But it does help us focus and move forward. Making the commitment toward a purpose-driven junior high ministry is a big step. It takes some work on the front end and, most likely, warrants the need to make a few changes in what you're currently doing.

To help you get started, you may want to evaluate your existing programs. It may hurt a little, but it's well worth the pain. Make a list of all the programs your ministry provides. Then, see if you can assign a biblical purpose to each one. Finally, ask yourself who you are hoping to reach with each program—who's the potential target?

There *is* more than one way to do this; no one way is the best. What's important is that you take the time to do so. Let me show you how we do it in our ministry to junior high students at Saddleback. It's not *the* way, but it is *a* way.

WHO	WHAT	HOW
are we trying to target?	is our purpose?	will we attempt to do this?
POTENTIAL TARGET	**PRIMARY PURPOSE**	**PRIMARY PROGRAM**
Care Less	Evangelism	Evangelism Ed. (peer evangelism)
Curious	Worship	Wildside Experience (weekend worship service)
Caught	Fellowship	Midweek C-groups (small groups)
Committed	Discipleship	Growing University (self-initiated discipleship tools)
Contagious	Ministry	Opportunities through ministry and missions to serve the body of Christ and the world

I'm really not interested in a big junior high ministry. I'm not interested in a flashy junior high ministry. I'm interested in a *healthy* junior high ministry. A healthy junior high ministry is one that understands God's biblical purposes for the church and is making an attempt to fulfill those purposes in the lives of students. Don't spend your time worrying about growth; spend it worrying about health—with health comes growth (for a much more in-depth study of this, be sure to read *Purpose-Driven Youth Ministry*).

CREATING PURPOSE-DRIVEN PROGRAMS FOR JUNIOR HIGH STUDENTS

One of the things I enjoy most about junior high ministry is creating programs. I love coming up with fun, interesting ways to fulfill the biblical purposes within our ministry setting. How you decide to fulfill the purposes in your ministry is up to you. The purposes of the church will never change, but how your ministry fulfills them may be in a state of constant change. I know ours is.

Let's take a look at some programs a healthy junior high ministry provides for its students.

A healthy junior high ministry provides opportunities for evangelism.

Evangelism is simply sharing the good news of Jesus Christ with those who don't have a relationship with him—reaching out to those who couldn't care less. A healthy junior high ministry is one that teaches students to care for and reach out to the lost and provides support to help them do so.

At Saddleback, our primary tool for outreach is our own students. We constantly challenge our students who have a relationship with

84

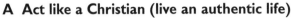

Christ to share him with others. We encourage students to follow a simple ABC plan of sharing Christ:

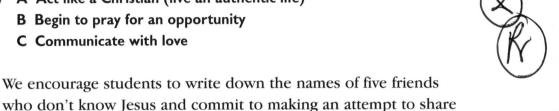

A Act like a Christian (live an authentic life)
B Begin to pray for an opportunity
C Communicate with love

We encourage students to write down the names of five friends who don't know Jesus and commit to making an attempt to share the good news with these friends through the ABCs.

In addition, our ministry provides two evangelistic programs each year. We do these only twice a year for two reasons: First, evangelistic programs are hard to maintain; they drain a huge chunk of time and resources. Second, we want students to own the responsibility of evangelism—it's their job more than it's ours. Instead of providing lots of evangelistic programs, we provide encouragement and tools to help students in their efforts to reach the lost.

Evangelism looks different in every ministry, but it must exist in order for your ministry to be healthy.

A healthy junior high ministry provides opportunities for worship.

Worship is much more than singing songs. We define worship as "celebrating God's presence and honoring him with our lifestyle." Romans 12:1 encourages us with these words,

> ". . . offer your bodies as living sacrifices, holy and pleasing to God—this is your spiritual act of worship."

Areas other than singing fall into this definition of worship. They include things like lifestyle choices, having a quiet time, memorizing Scripture and giving to support the work of the ministry. Because we use a broader definition, everything we do in our junior high ministry can be an act of worship, if it's holy and pleasing to God.

We have chosen to make our weekend service our primary program for giving students the opportunity to experience worship. Our junior high ministry is called "Wildside"; our weekend program is called the "Wildside Experience." We want it to be just that—an *experience* in worship. Here's what a typical Wildside Experience looks like:

WILDSIDE EXPERIENCE–SUNDAY 11:30 A.M.

11:35–11:45 A.M.	Fun, fast music with band
11:45–11:55 A.M.	Student challenge (silly game for prizes)
11:55–12:05 P.M.	Slower music with band
12:05–12:10 P.M.	Welcome and gifts given to guests
12:10–12:20 P.M.	Group game or video element
12:20–12:25 P.M.	Student testimony or talent
12:25–12:45 P.M.	Lesson

At every Wildside Experience, all five "target" students will be in attendance. This doesn't create a conflict because everyone can benefit from experiencing an atmosphere that honors God. Our committed and contagious students may value it more than the others, but everyone benefits from the experience.

We're constantly evaluating and changing our ministry's approach to worship. It's a challenge, but a healthy junior high ministry strives to provide opportunities for students to experience worship.

A healthy junior high ministry provides opportunities for fellowship.

The word "fellowship" is a lot like a football at the beach—it gets thrown around a lot, but with little accuracy. In the church, the word "fellowship" is used to describe all

Don't mistake video games and pizza parlors for true fellowship.

sorts of stuff. Throwing a pizza party is "fellowship." Volunteers stick around after the training meeting to "fellowship." We plan a day trip to the beach or zoo to offer students an opportunity to "fellowship." These activities are great, but they don't present an accurate picture of what is meant by New Testament fellowship.

Fellowship in the early church wasn't activity-driven. In the New Testament, Christians experienced fellowship by sharing life with one another. Fellowship included such things as sharing (1 John 1:7), breaking bread with other believers (Acts 2:42) and developing intima-

Be patient. Developing biblical fellowship takes time.

cy with each other (Galatians 2:9). I'm sure if the early followers of Christ had access to video games and pizza parlors they would have taken advantage of them, but not at the expense of true biblical fellowship.

Am I suggesting you try to create an atmosphere of sharing, intimacy and community in a junior high group? I am. I'm not saying it's an easy task, but if we want to create a healthy ministry to junior high

87

students, we need to provide an opportunity for those students who have been caught by Christ to experience the benefits of belonging to the body of Christ.

In our ministry, we've found that the best atmosphere for this to happen is in a small group setting. In small groups, relationships are built, walls break down, struggles are revealed and prayer requests are shared. In a small group setting, New Testament fellowship begins to emerge.

Our small groups are made up of students of the same grade and gender. They usually consist of no more than ten students and one or two adults. Our small groups meet once a week in the home of one of the participants. There are all sorts of ways to organize small groups. This has proven to work best in our setting. Here's what a typical small group meeting in our ministry looks like:

MIDWEEK SMALL GROUP MEETING

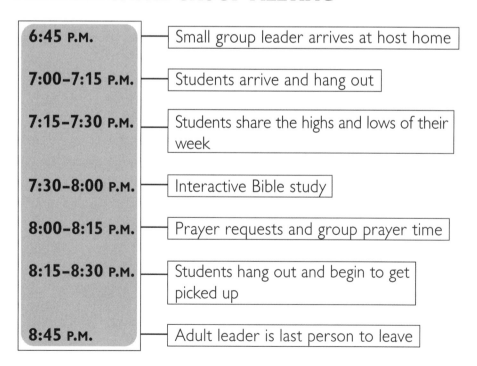

6:45 P.M.	Small group leader arrives at host home
7:00–7:15 P.M.	Students arrive and hang out
7:15–7:30 P.M.	Students share the highs and lows of their week
7:30–8:00 P.M.	Interactive Bible study
8:00–8:15 P.M.	Prayer requests and group prayer time
8:15–8:30 P.M.	Students hang out and begin to get picked up
8:45 P.M.	Adult leader is last person to leave

What about football? Play a lot of football! Spend lots of time playing video games, soccer and roller hockey with your small group (or whatever your group likes to do). Just be sure that you don't let these things take the place of biblical fellowship.

By now you probably know what I'm going to say, but let me say it anyway. You don't need to do small groups the way we do—you don't need to do small groups at all. However, a healthy junior high ministry will provide regular opportunities for students to experience biblical fellowship.

A healthy junior high ministry provides opportunities for discipleship.

Discipleship involves strengthening believers and helping them grow in Christlikeness. Hebrews 6:1 challenges us to ". . . leave the elementary teachings about Christ and go on to maturity." Discipleship is the process of growing spiritually.

A healthy junior high ministry provides opportunities for committed students to grow. This often takes place within the context of a Sunday school class, a small group setting or a one-on-one mentoring program. These traditional models of discipleship are time-tested and have proven to be very effective. However, there are two potential problems that can arise with these types of discipleship. First, they are high maintenance in nature. It takes an incredible amount of time, energy and commitment for adults to disciple students. Since junior high ministries are already asking for adult help in lots of other areas, it can be tough to make an additional plea for such a commitment.

LISTEN UP!

"I like the games and stuff, but I really go to church because it helps me realize that I'm not the only junior higher who thinks Jesus is cool."

—Amanda, eighth grade

Second, students often become dependent upon the program or the adult mentor for spiritual growth. If the program is discontinued or the adult moves on, discipleship in the student's life often comes to a stop.

At Saddleback, we give students tools to help them grow on their own. We call our discipleship program "Growing University." Growing University is a set of self-paced discipleship tools that encourage spiritual growth in students. To enroll in Growing University, a student simply picks up one of six Growing University "courses." Courses offered include Scripture Ed., Quiet Time Ed., Giving Ed., Evangelism Ed., Worship Ed. and Ministry Ed. On their own time, and at their own pace, students begin to develop habits that every mature Christian should be practicing. Our hopes are that we will equip students with habits they can take along life's road wherever their journey happens to take them.

Our approach to discipleship has its share of shortcomings. It isn't one-hundred percent effective in growing students to maturity in Christ—it may not even be seventy-five percent effective. But, two things our discipleship program has going for it are that it doesn't rely on a high maintenance program and it doesn't depend on adults.

Let me say one more time that *how* you do it isn't important. What is important is recognizing that in order to have a healthy junior high ministry you need to provide opportunities for discipleship.

A healthy junior high ministry provides opportunities for ministry.

Each year, a group of your junior high students move on to high school. Providing opportunities for ministry in junior high helps you graduate contagious ministers rather than mere attendees.

Junior high students are naturally selfish. This is partly because of the nature of early adolescence and all the changes and insecurities that go along with it. Most junior high students are worried enough about how *they'll* make it through the week; everybody else is on their own.

Another reason junior highers are selfish is because they have grown up in a selfish society. Yes, our society does have its share of do-gooders and charities, but as a whole it teaches us to reach for the stars, climb the ladder and grab a piece of the pie. When you combine who a junior higher is and the type of world he lives in, it's easy to see why ministering to others isn't at the top of his priority list.

It's important for junior high students to recognize that God has given them unique gifts that he hopes will be used to minister to others. A healthy junior high ministry needs to provide opportunities for students to discover their gifts and use them in service to the church and the world.

We do this by providing students with a variety of ministry opportunities. In our ministry, students can play in the band, be a greeter, work the Wildside booth, go on missions trips, share their testimony or talent, volunteer in the office, help with a children's Sunday school class . . . almost anything. Instead of creating ministry teams, we simply provide ministry opportunities and allow students to try them out. If a student wants to help us make a video, great! If she decides she doesn't like making videos and wants to try being a greeter, great! If she realizes that she isn't a people person, great! We'll use her to stack chairs. We try not to pigeonhole students into a particular ministry. Instead, we encourage them to jump around until they find their fit.

In Scripture, God has given us his purposes for the church—evangelism, worship, fellowship, discipleship and ministry. Building a junior high ministry that strives to fulfill these biblical purposes isn't an easy task. It's easier to simply hold our finger in the wind and "go with the flow." I don't trust my finger or the "flow." Instead of following the latest fads and gimmicks, a healthy junior high ministry is built around God's unchanging biblical purposes.

CHEW ON THIS

one

Ask two or three of your key volunteers this question: "Why does our junior high ministry exist?" Record their answers.

two

Which biblical purposes are found in the responses of your leaders? Did any of them include all five?

three

Look over your junior high ministry roster. Which students would you identify as curious? Which ones are caught, committed or contagious?

four Spend some time evaluating your current programs. What purpose does each of them fulfill? What audiences are they targeting? What biblical purposes are not being fulfilled in your ministry?

five On a scale of 1 to 10, how well is your ministry balancing the five purposes?

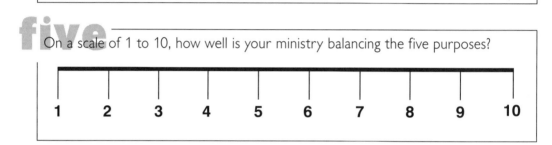

1   2   3   4   5   6   7   8   9   10

six What are some "next steps" you can take to improve balancing the purposes?

CHAOTIC THOUGHTS

"Preach the gospel at all times and, if necessary, use words." —Saint Francis of Assisi

CHAPTER SIX

PRESENTING THE GOOD NEWS

That's it . . . everything you need to know about how to teach, preach and communicate to junior high students. I don't think Saint Francis had us in mind when he said it, but the above quote could be the single most important piece of advice ever given to junior high workers. Okay, that's an overstatement, but it does merit some consideration.

I take a twofold approach to communicating to junior high students: The Things and The Talks.

BRAINWAVES
Students learn all the time . . .
not just during your lesson.

THE THINGS

A mistake junior high groups often make is the compartmentalization (that's the longest word I've ever typed!) of the teaching time. Let me explain. Everything your junior high ministry does should be viewed by the leadership of your ministry as a potential teaching time. Students learn all the time, not just during the 20 minutes you've scheduled into your Wednesday night program for the lesson or during Sunday school. We'll discuss later how to make the most out of the time you set aside for teaching, but it's important to recognize that everything that happens in the context of your junior high ministry is, in fact, teaching something to your students—even if you aren't saying a word.

In the following chart, I've listed a few "things" that may happen in the context of a typical junior high ministry and what each one may communicate to your students.

JUNIOR HIGH MINISTRY "THINGS" AT GENERIC COMMUNITY CHURCH

THING	LESSON
Visitors treated in a warm way	"God cares about lost people."
Adults interact with students	"They actually like us!"
Students involved in ministry	"God has gifted me."
Junior-high-friendly music	"At least they're trying."
Grace shown to troublemaker	"They'll forgive me."
Youth worker caught kissing spouse	"I didn't know old people still did that."
Consistency	"I can trust them."
Organization	"We're important to them."

Obviously, this list is just the tip of the iceberg. There are hundreds of things that happen in the junior high ministry setting that are, in fact, lessons to your students—even if you didn't intend for them to be. On the negative side, things like inconsistency, lack of organization, lack of grace and lack of student involvement also communicate to your students. But, is it the message you want to communicate?

LISTENUP!

"The best part about our lessons are the funny stories. I can't believe my youth pastor was so weird . . . how embarrassing!"

—Kyle, eighth grade

Here's something to think about. It's not profound, but it makes sense. Even though I'm the junior high pastor, I'm only a small part of the teaching team. Our teaching team is made up of every single "thing" that takes place in our ministry (like the stuff in the chart). Suppose we take a trip to the beach. As much as I like to hear myself talk, I'm smart enough to know not to try to give a twenty-minute lesson in that setting. However, the teaching team of "things" is going strong. We're organized enough to have a check-in list and extra permission slips ready for parents. There's plenty of transportation. Once we're at the beach, volunteers are bodysurfing with students, playing catch with them, asking them about their week, building relationships, etc. The lunch arrives somewhat on time, and we get home when we say we will. All day long, students have seen the good news of Christ lived out in the little things, which has far more impact than simply hearing about it during a twenty-minute talk.

"Actions speak louder than words." We've heard that truism all our lives. The "things" are the actions of your junior high ministry which, for better or worse, speak much louder than your words.

THE TALKS

I'm not sure what the setting will be. It may be in a small group of eighth-grade girls. It may be at the Friday night outreach event. It may be in front of the seventh-grade boys Sunday school class (GULP!). It may be in front of the entire group at your midweek program. I don't know when it will happen, or in what setting, but I can guarantee you this: It will happen. It's almost impossible to be involved in junior high ministry for any length of time without eventually having the opportunity to teach. I know that for some, the "opportunity" to swim in shark-infested waters sounds more appealing than it does for others. However, when you pause to think about it, teaching a group of young teenagers is an incredible opportunity that few people are given.

Teaching a group of young teenagers is an incredible opportunity that few people are given.

I love to teach. Of all my responsibilities as a junior high pastor, the responsibility, or opportunity, to speak to junior high students on a regular basis is one of the things I most enjoy. It's also something I feel fairly effective doing. It's not because I'm an incredibly gifted teacher. It's not because I'm the world's funniest guy. It's not even because I have the wisdom of Solomon. None of these is true about me.

I enjoy teaching, and am somewhat effective doing so because I've come to view it as an incredible opportunity that should be taken seriously. In Ephesians 5:16, Paul says,

"Make the most of every opportunity for doing good in these evil days" (NLT).

Successful teaching happens by determination, not by default.

When we are given the opportunity to communicate God's Word to junior high students, whatever the setting may be, we need to heed Paul's advice and make the most of it. Because I try to make the most out of every teaching opportunity, these times are usually a source of encouragement to my students and to me. I said *usually*, not *always*. Not every talk I give or small group discussion I lead goes smoothly. Let's face it, junior highers can be a tough crowd . . . in fact, they're probably the toughest crowd! There are times during my lessons that I feel as if I truly am swimming in shark-infested waters.

I'm risking taking the whole shark analogy a little too far, but here we go. I think the question that surfaces when we are in a teaching setting is this: "How do I feed the sharks without getting bit?" In other words, is it really possible to communicate to junior high students in a way that keeps both you and your group healthy and hungry for more? The answer is yes.

Successful teaching, however, doesn't happen by default. It happens by determination. You can be an effective teacher, but you have to be willing to put in the effort.

It's important to understand that the most vital part of any teaching situation is you, the teacher. At the heart of everyone, students and adults—anyone who has ever listened to a lesson, seminar, workshop or infomercial—are three basic questions: "Can I trust this person?", "Does this person know what he or she is talking about?" and "Of what interest is this to me?" Your goal as a teacher is to get to the point where your students trust you, think you know what you're talking about and are interested in what you have to say.

Videotape your lesson time once in awhile and evaluate yourself the next day.

GAINING TRUST

Here are a few quick ways you can gain the trust of your students. Notice that most of this is done before you ever step up front or get into your small group lesson plan.

THE 100% NONSCIENTIFIC STUDY ON HOW TO ~~GAIN THE TRUST~~ OF JUNIOR HIGH STUDENTS

Be involved long-term.

Students in eighth grade will more quickly trust leaders they've known since seventh grade.

Be yourself.

Students can smell a fake.

Be consistent.

Students can smell a flake.

Be vulnerable.

Students trust people who are willing to share their failures and struggles.

Be fair.

Life isn't fair, but junior high students think it should be.

BRAINWAVES

How you lead your life is more important than how you lead your lesson.

LISTENUP!

"I like it when they use demonstrations to show us what they're talking about."
—Tyler, eighth grade

When you're busy telling students what they *want* to hear, the issue of trust isn't all that important. When the time comes for you to address your students individually or as a group in areas that are challenging, stretching, uncomfortable or just plain unpopular, their trust in you is perhaps your greatest asset. For example, when I'm telling a student with ear, eyelid, nose, tongue, lip and navel piercings that God is more concerned with the heart than the appearance, my message is well received. He doesn't need to trust me to believe me; I've told him something he wants to hear. But if I begin to challenge that student's reasons for his appearance and how they may, in fact, be a reflection of his heart, it's a different story. That's probably not something my multi-pierced pal wanted to hear. However, if he trusts me, he's more likely to let my words pierce his heart (pun intended).

GAINING KNOWLEDGE

Here's some good news: If your junior high students trust you, they'll likely believe most of the stuff you tell them. After all, you are older and smarter than they are. Here's some other news: Your students are probably smarter than you give them credit for. For the first time in their lives, junior high students are beginning to ask questions like "Why?", "Who says?", "So what?" and "Prove it!" in their minds as they listen and learn.

The eight-year-old believes you because you are the teacher. The 13-year-old believes you because he trusts you and you know what you're talking about. While it isn't necessary to hold a doctorate in theology to be an effective junior high communicator, it is important to be a few steps ahead of your students in your knowledge of the Word of God and the world in which we live.

Here are a few simple ways to gain knowledge that will be useful to you as a teacher of junior high students:

GAINING KNOWLEDGE MADE SIMPLE

Determine to be a lifelong learner.

Be committed to personal Bible study.

Subscribe to publications geared for youth workers (such as *Group* magazine and *Youthworker* Journal).

Convince your church to send you to one training seminar a year.

Ask a more-experienced youth worker to mentor you (I am mentored monthly by Don Thompson, a 25-year veteran volunteer).

Spend time on the Internet.

Network with other youth workers.

Read books (congratulations!).

GAINING INTEREST

In high school or college, who was your favorite teacher? If everyone reading this book were to get together (hopefully we wouldn't all fit in my living room!) and compare notes about our favorite teachers, I think we would find a common denominator. Our favorite teachers probably weren't just trustworthy and knowledgeable alone. In fact, some of my least favorite teachers were the ones who seemed the smartest. I think what separates our favorite teachers from the rest of the pack is their ability to make us want to learn—to make learning interesting.

I'm going to go out on a limb, step on a few toes, ruffle a few feathers and stir up the pot for a few minutes. Really, I'm not the kind of guy looking for a reason to mess with the status quo, but I think this is a battle worth fighting. As junior high youth workers, you and I have bought a lie. We've been told that the attention span of young teenagers is only 10-15 minutes. I tend to agree with that. The lie isn't that junior highers have a short attention span. The lie is that we need to keep their attention.

BRAINWAVES

The more interested a student, the longer his attention span.

Right about now, you're thinking the limb I'm on is about to break, but hear me out. It's not about keeping their attention; it's about keeping their interest. While junior highers may have a short attention span, I think their interest span is much longer.

When I see a restored '57 Chevy on the street, it catches my attention. But because I'm not very interested in cars, my attention quickly shifts. The key to getting me to take a long look at the car and go home and tell my family about it is for something to increase my interest in old cars.

Think about infomercials. Why are these long, drawn-out advertisements so successful? They aren't the most high-budget ads on television, they aren't filled with incredible effects, music and photography. They aren't even shot in exotic locations. Why do infomercials work? Because they are effective in increasing the interest of viewers in the product.

BRAINWAVES

When God's Word is made interesting, students develop a hunger for it.

It's easy to get junior highers' attention—just be loud and flashy. The problem is there's always something louder or more flashy on the horizon. Your goal as a teacher is higher than simply keeping their attention. Your objective is to increase their interest in the things of God. If you can increase their interest in what you have to say, you won't have trouble keeping their attention.

I realize this is easier said than done, that a good chunk of our students aren't the least bit interested in spiritual things . . . or so it seems. I think that Bible study in itself probably doesn't grab the attention of most junior high students. I do think, though, that when God's Word is made interesting, students develop a hunger for it.

Let's recap a few things. We need to make the most out of every opportunity we have to teach. Our favorite teachers were those who made learning interesting. In case you're still not tracking with me, allow me to connect the dots for you: Making the most out of your teaching opportunities includes the willingness to make learning interesting.

"Wait just one minute," you may be saying. "God's Word doesn't need any help—it stands alone." You're absolutely right. In fact, Hebrews 4:12 tells us this:

> *"For the word of God is living and active. Sharper than any double-edged sword, it penetrates even to dividing soul and spirit, joints and marrow; it judges the thoughts and attitudes of the heart."*

God's Word is powerful stuff! I'm not saying God's Word needs to be made more interesting. I'm saying we need to make students more interested in God's Word.

One of my favorite teachers in junior high was my Spanish teacher, Mr. Duncan. He wasn't my favorite because he made the Spanish language more interesting. Frankly, when I was in junior high the only language interesting to me was "foul." (Got any kids like that in your group?) Mr. Duncan was one of my favorite teachers because he did things that made me more interested in learning the Spanish language.

"I like the lessons a lot more when I stay awake."
—Drew, seventh grade

You can go to any Christian bookstore or visit almost any publisher's website and find entire books dedicated to creative ways to communicate to students. If you can think of a wacky, attention-grabbing idea, you're too late because someone else already thought of it and put it in book form. I own those books and I love them! My most dog-eared books include these titles: *Magnetic Teaching*, by Rick Bundschuh; *Everyday Object Lessons*, by Helen Musick and Duffy Robbins; *How to Speak to Youth*, by Ken Davis; and the Ideas Library published by Youth Specialties. These books and dozens like them are full of ideas that not only grab your students' attention, but will help you develop an interest in their minds and spark your own creativity.

I recommend you fill your library with books like those, but because I want this book to be the most dog-eared in your collection, I'm going to enumerate some of my favorite interest-increasing tools. It's important to recognize that not every student in your group learns the same way. Incorporating a variety of communication methods in your lessons will help reach a variety of students.

Storytelling

Jesus' method of choice. Nothing beats stories. You can find them in illustration books or better yet, use stories from your own life (this helps build trust). There are some great books out on the market filled with stories for students. Among them are *Jawdroppers: 36 Shocking Stories for Students Based on the Sayings of Jesus*, by Steven James; and the *Hot Illustrations for Youth Talks* books (which include several volumes).

Object lessons

Use them two ways:
1. You can build an entire lesson around the object.
2. While prepping your lesson, ask yourself if there is an object you can use to make a particular point more interesting.

Clips

Using relevant, appropriate clips from television or movie videos is a great way to introduce a topic or illustrate a point. There are sev-

eral great books that have categorized tons of these, including *Videos That Teach*, by Doug Fields and Eddie James, and *Group's Blockbuster Movie Illustrations*, by Bryan Belknap. Use their ideas as a springboard to get you started. A couple of websites that are great resources for this are www.youthministry.com/m_m/ and www.nappaland.com.

Dialogue

Even in large settings, I like to get student feedback or have them turn to someone for a few minutes to discuss a given topic.

Case studies

An oldie but goodie. Students love to discuss the "What would you do?" scenarios found in case studies.

Planned interruptions

In the middle of a talk have someone rudely interrupt you in any

It doesn't have to be long to be good, but if it's going to be long, it'd better be good!

number of ways. We've had special deliveries, fake arguments, people getting up and walking out and people hopping out from backstage, among other things. Steal some of the ideas you've seen on "The David Letterman Show."

Role plays

Allow students to play out a given scenario by assigning them parts and asking them to perform their roles. For example: Three students play the parts of a mom, a dad and a daughter discussing her lack of effort at school.

Series teaching

I enjoy teaching in series form. A series is sort of like an infomercial. It doesn't have to hit 'em all at once. I can take my time and draw them in over two or three weeks. Plus, a series allows you to explore a given topic more thoroughly.

Curriculum

Use it, but customize it to fit your specific setting. I think curriculum is one of the greatest inventions ever. Unless you have an extra ten hours a week, why are you writing your own material? My favorite curriculum providers are David C. Cook, Standard Publishing, Empowered Youth Products, Group and Youth Specialties. Chances are your denominational headquarters also produces curriculum that is available at a reasonable rate.

PowerPoint®

Use PowerPoint® presentations to enhance your talks. Photos, graphics, video clips, Scripture verses and lesson outlines can all be put into a PowerPoint® presentation to enhance your talk and heighten the interest of your students.

Mix it up

Last but definitely not least, remember to mix it up! Just because your students love object lessons doesn't mean you should use them every week. If students always know what to expect, they will lose interest. Mix up your teaching style. Mix up your teachers. Mix up your topics (just because it's Easter doesn't mean you have to teach on the resurrection). Mix, mix, mix, mix, mix. Variety is the spice of life.

Do your students trust you? Do you have some knowledge about what you plan to teach? Do you have the desire and ability to help increase their interest in your topic? I hope so, because chances are your next teaching opportunity is only days away.

Let me give you a few things to think about as you prepare your next lesson. You probably won't agree with all of these tips, but they seem to work for me.

C TEACHING 101

The first minute is the most important minute.

It doesn't need to be long to be good.

If it's going to be long, it needs to be good.

Students like to laugh.

Students like stories.

Be real.

Be relevant.

When possible, include active learning ingredients. Students learn more when they experience it.

Offer specific application steps.

The last minute is also the most important minute.

The world is screaming its philosophies and messages to our students with seemingly endless energy. It seems to have unlimited resources at its disposal. The world will say, spend or do anything necessary to prick the ears of our students. How can we possibly combat that kind of pull on the hearts of our students? The best way I know is to believe that the

gospel of Jesus Christ is, in fact, good news to a hurting world. That motivates me to make the most out of every opportunity I have to present the truth.

CHEW ON THIS

one Compile a list of the "things" in your ministry. What messages, good or bad, are they sending to your students?

two Take a look at the tips for gaining the trust of junior high students. Which things on this list come naturally for you? Which ones take extra effort?

three What is one purposeful thing you can do to help yourself gain knowledge?

four Brainstorm five ideas you can implement into your teaching to heighten the interest of your students.

five On a scale of 1 to 10, how much effort do you put into preparing your talks or lessons?

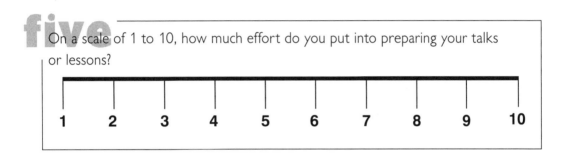

1   2   3   4   5   6   7   8   9   10

CHAOTIC THOUGHTS

CHAPTER SEVEN

PURPOSELY FUN

Find a hundred junior high students who like going to church and ask them why they enjoy it. Most of them will reply, "Because it's fun." Find a hundred junior high students who don't like going to church and ask them why they don't enjoy it. Most of them will echo Woody Allen's words.

Fun is the universal language of junior highers. Most junior high students don't come to church because of the spiritual growth they experience or the incredible worship times. They don't even come because of the creative lessons. There is only one gauge that determines whether or not a junior high student enjoys going to church: the "Fun O' Meter." How fun a student thinks church is going to be radically affects how excited he is about going.

BRAINWAVES

Fun is the universal language of junior highers.

A sterile, boring junior high ministry will likely attract only two types of students: those who are so in love with Jesus they'll put up with anything and those who are forced by their parents to show up. Creating an atmosphere of fun will help you

You don't have to be funny to create fun.

minister more effectively to the students you already have, and it will help you attract new students and families to your ministry.

It's important to define fun. Although silliness, humor and laughter are benefits in junior high ministry, you don't have to be funny to create fun. While funny is something that makes you laugh, *fun* is something that is enjoyable. For example, I have fun when I surf—I enjoy it. However, surfing isn't funny. I don't find myself chuckling under my breath or trying to contain my laughter when I surf. Others chuckle under their breath and try to contain their laughter when I surf, but that's an entirely different illustration!

Wild, crazy, high-energy games have their place in junior high ministry, and we'll talk about that later, but they aren't what makes a junior high ministry fun. Not everything that takes place at your midweek program, in the Sunday school class or on the mission trip is going to be considered funny, silly, wild, crazy or high energy. Each of these can, however, have a fun atmosphere, creating an environment that junior high students enjoy.

Here are four elements that help create an atmosphere of fun in a junior high ministry:

A FUN JUNIOR HIGH MINISTRY IS . . .
RELATIONAL
REAL
RELEVANT
RELAXED

RELATIONAL

Few things matter as much in the day-to-day lives of junior highers as their friendships. Despite this fact, many junior high ministries fail to take advantage of the natural desire for junior high students to develop relationships.

LISTENUP!

"When I know church is going to be fun, it makes me want to bring a friend."
—Micah, seventh grade

A fun junior high ministry is one that allows interaction, discussion and experience among friends—one that creates opportunities for students to strengthen their existing friendships and create new ones. Students enjoy hanging out with one another and with caring adults. Relational junior high ministry looks something like this:

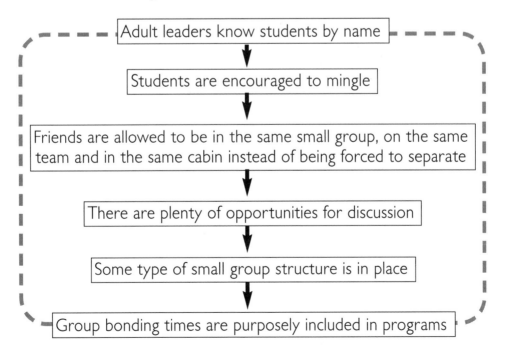

RELATIONAL JUNIOR HIGH MINISTRY

Adult leaders know students by name

↓

Students are encouraged to mingle

↓

Friends are allowed to be in the same small group, on the same team and in the same cabin instead of being forced to separate

↓

There are plenty of opportunities for discussion

↓

Some type of small group structure is in place

↓

Group bonding times are purposely included in programs

Real

When I was in junior high there was only one brand of clothing—at least that's what we all thought. To wear anything other than OP (Ocean Pacific) was committing sacrilege. Especially popular were the corduroy pants with the OP logo stitched on the front pocket. My mom had a problem with OP. Ocean Pacific pants cost $20 per pair and that was about $15 more than my mom was willing, or able, to spend. My mom's problem with OP quickly became my own.

One Saturday afternoon my mom returned from an outing at the Swap Meet. You might call it a flea market, but in our town it was the Swap Meet—the place you went to get good deals on everything from A to Z. My mom eagerly handed me a bag and told me to look inside. I can still remember the expectant look on her face as I reached inside the bag and pulled out a pair of navy blue, corduroy GW pants. I knew this because on the pocket where there should have been an "OP" was stitched a big golden "GW." Like I said, my mom's problem with OP quickly became my own. The GW stood for "Golden Wave," a Swap Meet version of OP. I was struck with terror. How could my mom possibly expect me to wear a pair of GW pants to school? Didn't she realize the humiliation I would face? She'd never make me wear 'em.

She made me wear 'em. It was humiliating. Somehow I lived through it.

"I like it when adults listen to me without jumping to conclusions. It makes me feel like I'm important to them."
—Sarah, eighth grade

In society, image is everything. Companies spend millions of dollars in an attempt to create an image that will sell their product. As a result, consumers buy products largely because of the image the product represents, with little regard to quality or value. The underlying message we've bought is this: "Don't let anyone see the real you; let them see only the image you've created."

Junior high students need a safe place, a place that doesn't put image on a pedestal; where it doesn't matter what brand of pants you wear. A fun junior high ministry is one where adult leaders create an atmosphere that allows students to be real—to be themselves. A fun junior high ministry is one that lets the cool kids be cool, the nerdy kids be nerdy, the shy kids be shy, the athletic kids be athletic, the clumsy kids be clumsy, the spiritual kids be spiritual and the skeptical kids be skeptical. Junior high students need a place that values the real, not the image.

Is this idealistic? Probably. Is it attainable? Possibly. Real junior high ministry looks something like this:

REAL JUNIOR HIGH MINISTRY

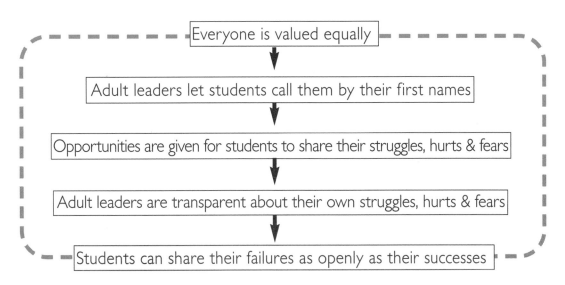

Everyone is valued equally

↓

Adult leaders let students call them by their first names

↓

Opportunities are given for students to share their struggles, hurts & fears

↓

Adult leaders are transparent about their own struggles, hurts & fears

↓

Students can share their failures as openly as their successes

RELEVANT

An interesting thing happens in early adolescence. Children who once believed almost everything they were told suddenly begin to question. They ask questions like "Who says?", "Why?" and "What does it mean to me?" Churchgoing six-year-olds don't question their faith—they believe in Christ because mom and dad believe in Christ and mom and dad know best.

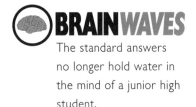

The standard answers no longer hold water in the mind of a junior high student.

Junior highers begin to question whether mom and dad really do know best. Junior highers who have always accepted the claims of Christianity as fact may now begin to question its relevance. The questions "Why?", "Who says?" and "What does it mean to me?" are directed to the church.

The standard answers like "because" and "we say so—that's why" no longer hold water in the mind of a junior high student. They need to be convinced for themselves. The goal of a junior high ministry isn't to fill the seats with students who are forced to be there because mom and dad "said so." The goal is to fill the seats with students who are beginning to think on their own, and on their own have decided that a relationship with Jesus is worth their time.

The effective junior high ministry is one that not only understands this, but embraces it. It is one that takes purposeful steps to create an atmosphere that allows junior highers to experience the relevance of Christ in their lives. I use the phrase "experience the relevance of Christ" because experience is exactly what it takes. Things of faith don't need more explaining; they need more experiencing. In short, junior high students need to own their own faith, and in order to own it, they must experience it.

Creating opportunities for students to experience their faith in action helps make a junior high ministry fun. Relevant junior high ministry looks something like this:

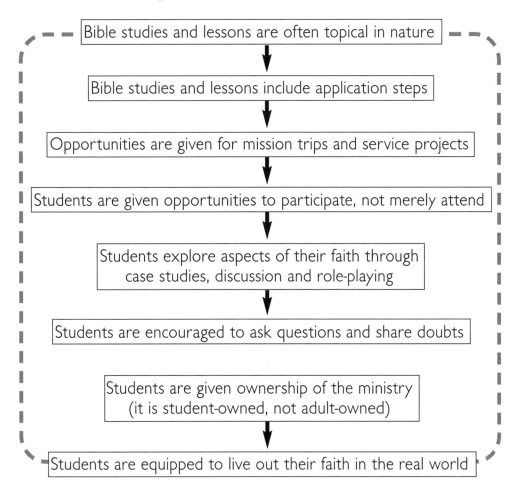

RELEVANT JUNIOR HIGH MINISTRY

Bible studies and lessons are often topical in nature

↓

Bible studies and lessons include application steps

↓

Opportunities are given for mission trips and service projects

↓

Students are given opportunities to participate, not merely attend

↓

Students explore aspects of their faith through case studies, discussion and role-playing

↓

Students are encouraged to ask questions and share doubts

↓

Students are given ownership of the ministry (it is student-owned, not adult-owned)

↓

Students are equipped to live out their faith in the real world

RELAXED

The only people who benefit from stress are cardiologists. It's our stress that keeps them in business. Unfortunately we live in a world that keeps them gainfully employed. Stress is part of everyone's life, and junior highers are no exception. It hasn't always been this way.

BRAINWAVES
The only people who benefit from stress are cardiologists.

When I was in junior high, I hadn't even thought about high school yet, let alone college. Today, junior high students are under pressure to take the right classes and get the right grades so they can take the right classes in high school. Then, if they get the right grades there, they may get into the college of their parents' choosing.

In my young teen years, I played baseball just for the fun of it. The season lasted about three months. Today, junior high students play baseball in order to better their chance of making the high school varsity team at a younger age. Many play baseball year-round so they will increase their odds of making this happen. They do all this because they might earn an athletic scholarship to the college of their parents' choosing.

BRAINWAVES
Today's junior highers live in a world that is much more stressful than it used to be.

When I was in junior high, campus violence was almost unheard of. Today, many students wonder if they'll live long enough to attend the college of their parents' choosing.

You want to know what my biggest stress was in junior high? I'll give you a hint: Navy blue, corduroy, GW.

Have I overstated things here? Yes I have . . . slightly. The truth of the matter is that today's junior high students live in a world that is much more stressful than it used to be. Teens today live in a world run by stressed-out adults. Parents seem more stressed. Teachers seem more stressed. Coaches seem more stressed (probably because they fear an attack by a mob of overstressed parents who are concerned about their children getting athletic scholarships to the college of their choosing). Junior high youth workers seem more stressed.

Life is stressful. I realize that. If you are a full-time junior high worker, I understand the pressures you face. If you are part-time or volunteer, I can only imagine that the pressures you face to balance family, career and ministry are multiplied several times.

It is no secret that life is stressful. But do yourself, your ministry and most importantly, your students a favor by leaving that stress behind when you enter the junior high room.

Junior highers like to have fun, but stress is no fun. Instead, work to create a relaxed environment that counteracts the stress and pressures junior highers face on a daily basis. Relaxed junior high ministry looks something like this:

RELAXED JUNIOR HIGH MINISTRY

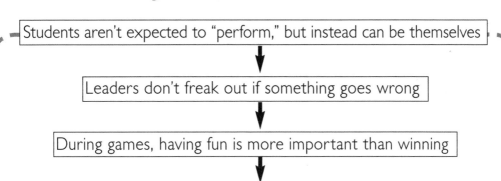

Students aren't expected to "perform," but instead can be themselves

Leaders don't freak out if something goes wrong

During games, having fun is more important than winning

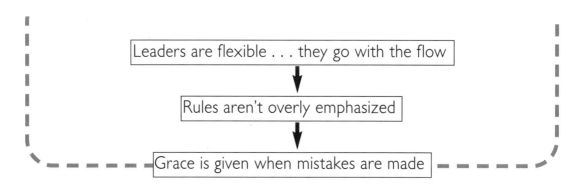

Leaders are flexible . . . they go with the flow

↓

Rules aren't overly emphasized

↓

Grace is given when mistakes are made

BRAINWAVES
Learn to laugh at yourself.
. . . everyone else is.

Remember, the definition of fun is something that is enjoyable. Even if you aren't the funniest person around, and even if your ministry isn't marked by the goopiest, gooeyist, grossest games in town, it can still be fun, as long as it is relational, real, relevant and relaxed.

But what about the games—the goopy, gooey, and often gross part of junior high ministry? Like I said before, you don't need them to have fun, but let's admit this: They are one of the best aspects of working with junior highers!

LISTENUP!
"I think church needs to be fun because most people think it isn't."
—Vanessa, eighth grade

I'm not going to list a bunch of new games. There are dozens of books and resources that can give you some help. Instead of focusing on *what* games to play, let's take a look at *how* to play them.

"Isn't every game played differently?" you may be asking. No. In fact, every game should be played exactly the same way. The way a game is played makes it fun—not the game itself.

HOW TO MAKE GAMES FUN

Be energetic.

If you're excited about a game, students will be too. An excited leader can get a group of junior high students excited about virtually any game—even one as cheesy as the Lifesaver/Toothpick relay.

THE BOTTOM LINE:

The energy of the staff will dictate the energy of the students.

Be organized.

Make sure you know how to play the game before you unleash it on your students. Be sure to gather the proper supplies ahead of time. If a student is going to get messy, bring a towel or change of clothes. If the rules of the game call for 50 balloons, make 75. If the game time is part of an ongoing team competition, be sure to correctly add points.

BRAINWAVES

The way a game is played makes it fun—not the game itself.

THE BOTTOM LINE:

Know what you're doing before you do it.

Be clear.

Simple, easy-to-understand games are the most effective. Games that take 20 minutes to explain and five minutes to play aren't much fun. When explaining the rules of a game, there are three good guidelines:

1. Keep them short.
2. Keep them simple.
3. Keep students quiet until you're finished.

THE BOTTOM LINE:

Confusing games create chaos.

Be fair.

Don't twist the scores so the eighth graders win. Don't invent rules halfway through the game. Don't give the seventh-grade girls a few "secret" tips. Junior high students are notorious for yelling, "That's not fair!" When it comes to game time, they're often right.

THE BOTTOM LINE:

Keep it fun by keeping it fair.

Be sensitive.

Don't use games to purposely embarrass students. Don't ridicule

Laughter is a natural by-product of fun junior high ministry.

their performance. Don't humiliate one student to get a laugh from the others. Don't force students to participate; they may actually have a good reason for not wanting to.

THE BOTTOM LINE:

Use games to build up, not tear down.

Be smart.

Quit while you're ahead. Always leave them wanting more. End each game on a high note. If a game is going poorly, quit before it turns disastrous! Here's a hot tip: Don't play a game that you would be uncomfortable playing in front of parents. If you think maybe you shouldn't . . . you shouldn't!

THE BOTTOM LINE:

It's always better to be safe than sorry!

Be willing to mix it up.

Not every student likes every type of game. In addition, not every student is adept at every type of game. Because of this, be sure to mix up the types of games you play. Strive for a balance between physical games, mental games, group games and individual games. If you limit the variety, you limit the interest and enthusiasm. Also, avoid the temptation to play students' favorite games too often. Their favorite game can quickly become their least favorite game if you play it every week. In our ministry, we try not to play the same game more than three times a year—no matter how popular it is.

THE BOTTOM LINE:
Don't get into a rut—even a good one.

Laughter is a natural by-product of fun junior high ministry. Really, we don't need to work too hard to create it because if junior highers are having fun, laughter is part of the picture. Although we don't need to create laughter, we often find ourselves trying to do just that. I'm not going to try to explain how to create laughter and be funny. You'll need to talk to a comedian about that. I do, however, want to wrap up this chapter by giving some insight into how *not* to create laughter and be funny. Keep these tips in mind as you plan games and create programs in an attempt to make your junior high ministry fun.

KURT'S PHILOSOPHY OF NOT FUNNY

IT'S NOT FUNNY IF
→ humor is at the expense of an individual ←

IT'S NOT FUNNY IF
→ it's degrading ←

IT'S NOT FUNNY IF
→ it's for "shock value" ←

IT'S NOT FUNNY IF
→ it undermines authority ←

IT'S NOT FUNNY IF
→ someone gets hurt ←

IT'S NOT FUNNY IF
→ you've overkilled it (less is more) ←

IT'S NOT FUNNY IF
→ no one's laughing ←

Too many churches provide a boring, dull approach to junior high ministry and expect junior highers to appreciate it. It's an unfair expectation. As adults, they'll have plenty of opportunities to experience boring, dull approaches to ministry. In fact, some of them will choose to attend seminary and will actually pay for a boring, dull approach to ministry.

While we have them, for these two or three short years, let's have some fun!

CHEW ON THIS

one What part of your junior high ministry do you think students find the most enjoyable? Why?

two Think through your various programs. What type of atmosphere is created by each one?

three Of the four characteristics of a fun junior high ministry, which one is most evident in you as an individual?

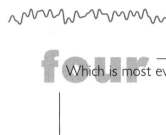

four Which is most evident in your ministry?

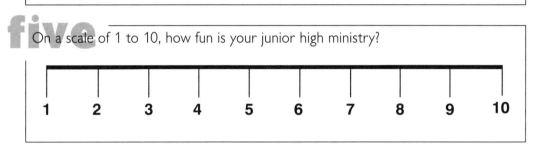

five On a scale of 1 to 10, how fun is your junior high ministry?

1   2   3   4   5   6   7   8   9   10

CHAOTIC THOUGHTS

CHAPTER EIGHT

POINTING THE WAY

One of the highlights of my ministry career was working for three years with John Maxwell in San Diego, California. While on his staff I learned that everything truly does rise and fall on leadership. Many people think that in junior high ministry, everything rises and falls on lock-ins, but there's more to a healthy youth ministry than the ability to run an event. Leadership is an essential part of a healthy junior high ministry. In this chapter we'll explore this vital topic.

I'm not sure how you came to be a leader in your junior high ministry. It could be that someone simply pointed at you and said, "Hey, you'd be a good junior high leader" and in a moment of weakness you agreed. It may have been a little more strategic than that, but since we're talking about junior high ministry . . . uh . . . it's unlikely.

Many of you reading this book are *the* leader of your junior high ministry. You are the person, whether full-time, part-time or volunteer, who has been given the reins. Most of you aren't *the* leader of the ministry, but, instead serve as *a* leader in the ministry. This

chapter is for you, too. I want to start by addressing the needs of *the* leader.

RESPONSIBILITIES OF THE LEADER:
HOW TO LEAD FROM THE FRONT

Point the way.

Where are we heading? What are our goals? What do we want to see accomplished in the lives of our students? Why do we exist as a ministry? How do we know we're successful? These are all essential questions every junior high ministry needs to ask. These are also questions the leader needs to answer. One of the primary roles of the leader is to do just that— lead! As the point person, you are expected to point the way so others can follow.

BRAINWAVES

The role of the leader is to decide which mountains the ministry climbs and which ones it doesn't.

An effective leader knows what needs to be accomplished, charts a course to get there, sets realistic goals to achieve along the way and evaluates the progress. In essence, it is the leader's responsibility to say, "Here's where we're heading, and I'm going to make sure that, together, we get there."

There's an old saying that says, "The reason the man climbed the mountain was simply because it was there." In junior high ministry, not every mountain needs to be climbed. Your ministry faces a large variety of opportunities and options, but it can do only so much. The role of the leader is to decide which mountains the ministry climbs and which ones it doesn't.

SELL Sell the vision.

I'm the proud owner of the world's most expensive gym membership. It's true. Three years ago I paid $400 for a lifetime membership to a local health club. At first glance, that seems like a pretty good deal. Here's the problem: I've used the gym only twice! That's right, over the past three years, I've gone to the gym exactly two times. I've paid two hundred dollars per workout! Here's what happened: I stopped by the gym on the way home from work and a slick, good-looking, young guy sold me on the vision of what my life would be like if I joined the gym. I'd have more energy. I'd feel better about myself. I'd look better. After spending about 15 minutes with the salesman, I had a vision of the new Kurt Johnston. (I would have paid $600 if he had told me I'd be taller, too). The new me would be an incredibly fit, healthy and confident man. I rushed out of the gym and headed home.

When I got there, I proceeded to sell the vision of the new me to my wife Rachel. Initially, she commented that she sort of liked the Kurt she had, but I eventually wore her down. The vision of a Kurt with muscles was more than she could handle. A week later I was the owner of what would turn out to be the world's most expensive gym membership—all because a slick salesman

BRAINWAVES

Write a purpose statement for your ministry and have the leadership team memorize it.

sold me on a vision. Now, people in your church might not be as dumb as me, but they do need someone to cast a vision if they're going to "buy" into your junior high ministry.

When we read about Nehemiah, we know he had a vision. The walls of Jerusalem had been destroyed and the city was in a state of disgrace. Nehemiah wanted to lead an effort to rebuild the city's walls. Having the desire to rebuild the walls wasn't what made him a leader; certainly other people felt the same way. What set him apart was his ability to sell the vision of a rebuilt wall to the king, the various governors and others who would eventually help. It would have been impossible to rebuild the walls alone. Nehemiah had to convince others that the project was "a mountain worth climbing."

One of the biggest responsibilities of being the leader is also one of the biggest joys: selling others on the vision. I hope you have a vision of what God wants to do in and through your ministry to junior high students. It's impossible for you to do it alone. Allow others to share the joy of seeing the vision fulfilled.

WHEN OTHERS BUY THE VISION

 They'll give their support (Nehemiah 2:5, 6).

 They'll give their help (Nehemiah 2:18).

 They'll give their hearts (Nehemiah 4:6).

EQUIP
Equip the troops.

Not only does the leader need to sell people on the vision of junior high ministry, he or she also needs to help them succeed in their efforts. As mentioned in chapter two, the primary role of the point person is to equip God's people for works of service. Here are five tips to help you equip others who are playing a leadership role on your team:

EMPOWER
Give freedom to minister and lead.

QUIETLY CORRECT
When correction is needed, do so privately.

UNLIMITED SUPPORT
Become their biggest cheerleader.

INVEST TIME
Follow Christ's example: he invested time with those carrying out his ministry.

PROVIDE TOOLS
Make sure training, seminars and resources are available.

My experience is that effective junior high ministry is more caught than taught. Look at the tips for equipping again. Notice that of the five, only one has to do with any type of structured training time.

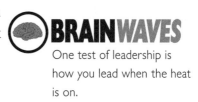
BRAINWAVES

One test of leadership is how you lead when the heat is on.

Make the decisions.

A key part of empowering others is permitting them to make decisions. As the leader of the ministry, you don't need to be involved in every decision made, but there are decisions that no one else should make. Certain decisions are the responsibility of the leader and it would be unfair and unwise to let others make them for the ministry. As the leader, it is your responsibility to make the tough decisions. Scripture encourages us to seek wise counsel, but ultimately, the decision needs to be made by the leader of the ministry. Here are some of the decisions I make in our ministry:

SOME DECISIONS OF

 Potential volunteers *(who's accepted and who's not)*

 Budget issues

 Student disciplinary situations

 Long-term vision

 Significant changes

Take the heat.

It's going to happen. I wish it didn't, but it does. Sooner or later your ministry is going to come under fire. Someone, somewhere will be unhappy about something that somehow went wrong.

Accusations will fly, rumors will spread and blame will need to be placed. One test of leadership is how you lead when the heat is on. Insecure leaders look for ways to pass the blame elsewhere. Healthy leaders are willing to take the heat for what happens in their ministry.

"I think a leader needs to know what he's doing, and keep a good attitude while he's doing it."

—Jessie, seventh grade

A few years ago we took a bunch of students to the Anaheim Pond to see an "Arena Football" game. We took a bunch of students to the game and returned with a bunch . . . minus one. After an exciting night of not-quite-ready-for-prime-time football, we headed for the parking lot. I had asked one of our leaders to be responsible for making the final head count before the buses headed for home. I always try to ask the same staff member (she's a real good counter).

When we arrived at the church parking lot, I was met by a furious father. His son Chris had called a few minutes earlier from the security office at The Pond. Somehow, we had managed to leave Chris at the game. His wife was on her way to pick Chris up, but dad wanted a few minutes of my time and a few ounces of my flesh. "How could this have happened . . . don't you know how to count?" he demanded. At that moment, everything in me wanted to point my finger at Katie, the woman I thought was a good counter. I didn't. I pulled the understandably upset father aside and let him chew me out for the next fifteen minutes. I listened as he called me irresponsible and immature. I nodded my head in agreement as he questioned my ability to lead young teens. I never let him know that it was someone else who had done the counting. Passing the blame wouldn't have made him feel any better and it wouldn't have eliminated the fact that we had made a mistake.

Because I'm the leader of our ministry to students, I'm responsible for everything that happens in our ministry. The next day Katie and I had a serious talk about her counting skills.

Why didn't I point the angry dad to Katie? Why didn't I let her take the heat as a leader for her mistake? Because Katie and all the other volunteers in our ministries deserve loyalty from their leader. Nothing will burn a volunteer out more than dealing with unhappy parents and unresolved problems. Most youth workers are involved with students because they like students. They didn't sign on because they wanted the opportunity to handle tough situations. By taking the heat, I not only protected Katie from an unpleasant encounter, I also earned her trust and loyalty.

As the leader of your ministry, you need to be willing to take the heat.

PASS **Pass the praise.**

Healthy leaders look for opportunities to pass the credit. If you're the leader of your ministry, chances are you get most of the credit.

Recently, a high school freshman and his dad came to visit me. In his hand the dad was carrying a gift. They gave it to me and asked me to open it. As I opened the gift, tears came to my eyes. In my hands was a Super Bowl XXXII football autographed by John Elway. Every student in our ministry knows that John Elway is my hero. Every football season, I wear my Elway jersey every Sunday until Denver loses its first game. I am possibly the world's greatest Denver Bronco trash talker.

Alek and his dad wanted to thank me for the incredible impact our junior high ministry had made in Alek's life. The football was the best way they could think of to say thanks. I wish I could take credit for Alek's experience in our ministry, but I can't. The reason he enjoyed his junior high years was really because of his small group leader, Will. Will spent every Tuesday night hanging out with Alek and his buddies. Will wrote him letters of encouragement. Will put up with his antics in the middle of their small group study. I did none of these things, yet I was holding the football.

I made sure to remind Alek and his dad about Will—that it was really Will who made Alek's junior high experience a life-changing one. I encouraged them to express their gratitude to Will. I did *not*, however, offer to give the football to Will. I'm the proud owner of a John Elway autographed football, not because I'm a good youth worker, but because Will is.

Since you already get some credit for things you do, and even for things you don't do, I encourage you to look for ways to start passing the praise around.

IDEAS FOR PASSING THE PRAISE

Create a "volunteer of the month" award.

Highlight team members' accomplishments in your church newsletter.

Host a volunteer appreciation banquet.

Give volunteers the freedom to miss an occasional program.

Pay for their dinner and a movie during their missed program.

Thank them for their commitment—after all, it's why you get special gifts!

BEAT.
Beat the drum.

Nobody should be as excited about the junior high ministry as much as you. Nobody should be talking about the ministry as much as you. Nobody should be thinking about the ministry as much as you. It's up to you to beat the drum of junior high ministry. Remind other leaders of your purposes and plans to get there, sell the vision on a regular basis to whomever will listen and keep other church leaders and departments updated on the junior high ministry. Beat the drum often and beat the drum loud (loud doesn't mean overbearing or obnoxious, but consistent)! If you're not doing it, chances are nobody else is.

OPPORTUNITIES OF
A LEADER:
HOW TO LEAD FROM THE MIDDLE

Let me spend some time with those of you who aren't *the* leader of your junior high ministry but are *a* leader in it. I'm not sure what your responsibilities to the ministry are but, chances are you have a variety of responsibilities and wear several different hats on a regular basis. You may be the only additional leader your ministry has, or you may be one of twenty.

Every once in a while, a volunteer in our ministry will ask questions like these: "How can I help you succeed?", "Is there anything extra you need from me?" or "Is there a larger role I can play in our ministry?"

BRAINWAVES

Words are powerful; use them to support your leader in front of others.

What these people are really asking is, "How can I become more of a leader in our ministry?" Even though these men and women know that they aren't *the* leader of our ministry, they want to take on some extra leadership responsibilities. In essence, they want to be leaders among leaders— they want to lead from the middle.

LISTENUP!

"Not every leader is popular, but I'll bet being popular helps."

—Nate, eighth grade

If you are *a* leader in your ministry who wants to lead from the middle, I'm thankful for you. Junior high ministries around the world need more people like you. Here are some opportunities that will help you become a leader among leaders.

Support your leader publicly.

It is tough to exaggerate the power of words. The book of James reminds us that the tongue is a powerful tool. It is the responsibility of the leader of your ministry to beat the drum, but take advantage of the opportunity to beat the drum with him. Publicly support the decisions made, the goals set and the direction taken. It's okay to disagree with your leader—but avoid doing so in public. Words are powerful; use them to support your leader in front of others.

Be consistent.

More valuable than being willing to take on extra things is consistently fulfilling the things you're already doing. We have a saying in our ministry: "Be committed to what you've committed to." I'm not interested in the youngest, coolest volunteer that may be here today and gone tomorrow. I want leaders around me who are consistent in the daily grind of junior high ministry. Someone who leads from the middle is someone who models consistency.

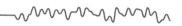

Go the extra mile.

Being consistent is worthy of applause. Being willing to go the extra mile deserves a standing ovation! Staying late after an activity to help clean up while other volunteers head to the movies is going the extra mile. Taking a week of vacation time to be a counselor in a cabin full of seventh-grade boys is going the extra mile. Opening your home for a Friday night sleepover is going the extra *two* miles!

Take some initiative.

Good volunteers do what they're asked to do. Really good volunteers ask what they can do. Incredible volunteers, those who lead from the middle, just do without asking.

Offset the weaknesses of the leader.

I have a few strengths and a bunch of weaknesses. I'm blessed to be surrounded by volunteer leaders who more than make up for my weaknesses. I'm not very organized, but Don Thompson is. I'm not a real good encourager, but Gary Eilts is. I'm not all that creative, but Allison Hibbard is. All three of these volunteers have proven to be leaders among our leaders. All three have made purposeful efforts to offset my weaknesses by using their strengths in our ministry. Don organizes our summer and winter camps. Gary shepherds our small group leaders. Allison serves on our weekend design team.

Your leader has a lot of weaknesses too. You'll bless his life by offsetting his weaknesses by using your strengths. Now, if he doesn't think he has any weaknesses, tell him to wake up and smell the coffee (or have him call me and I'll do that for you)!

SPREAD
Spread the word.

People expect the leader of your ministry to talk about it. After all, he or she is the one who should be beating the drum more often and louder than anyone else. What people don't expect is for other adults to talk about the junior high group. Share what God's doing in the junior high group with your adult Sunday school class. Tell the choir about your experience as a small group leader. Track down the senior pastor and let him know how fulfilled you are serving in the junior high ministry.

BRAINWAVES

One of the biggest assets a leader has is longevity.

STICK
Stick around awhile.

One of the biggest assets a leader has is longevity. Tim Walker is a volunteer in our ministry. This year, Tim will celebrate his tenth anniversary in the junior high department at Saddleback. Amazing! Tim supports me publicly, is consistent, goes the extra mile, takes initiative, offsets my weaknesses and spreads the word about our ministry. But what makes him a key leader among our leaders is that he's been around for ten years. He knows the history of our ministry. He's seen families send their oldest, middle and youngest children through our doors. He's done junior high ministry in school cafeterias, movie theaters, portable buildings and tents. He's endured the grandiose visions and plans of numerous full-time leaders. Yet, ten years later Tim is still sticking around. Longevity alone won't make you a leader among leaders, but when it's coupled with the other qualities, it makes you a guru!

Thanks for being a leader in your church's ministry to junior high students. You may even be *the* leader. In any case, I hope this chapter has pointed you toward some of the responsibilities and opportunities that await you.

Finally, let me put all this into the context we're most familiar with: Someone has to make the decision to have a balloon relay next week. Someone else needs to plan it. Someone also needs to be willing to take the heat if it goes poorly and pass the praise if it's a success. Others need to be ready to publicly defend the decision to have a balloon relay in the first place. Still others need to go the extra mile and pick up all those tiny pieces of broken balloons!

Thanks for being that someone!

CHEW ON THIS

one Look at each of the _seven_ _responsibilities_ of _the_ leader. Write down a personal experience for each one.

two Write down three ways that you will pass the praise on to someone else this month.

three

Look at each of the _seven opportunities_ of _a_ leader. Write down a personal experience for each one.

four

Write down three ways you will go the extra mile this month.

five

On a scale of 1 to 10, how well do you lead from the position you're in (the front or the middle)?

| 1 | 2 | 3 | 4 | 5 | 6 | 7 | 8 | 9 | 10 |

CHAOTIC THOUGHTS

CHAPTER NINE

PERSEVERANCE
(How to hang in there for the long haul)

When I was in junior high, my friends and I would often go to the Swap Meet on Saturday mornings (Swap Meets were a big thing in my family). In the middle of all the booths selling fish, flashlights and Farrah Fawcett posters was a unique exhibit. At this booth, curious bystanders paid $1.00 to climb up a ladder and look into an enclosed cage that housed "the world's strangest animal." The line was always long. The routine was always the same: Curious bystander pays $1.00. Curious bystander climbs ladder and looks into cage. Curious bystander is shocked by what he sees. Curious bystander gasps once or twice. Operator of booth asks curious bystander if he would like to touch the animal. Curious bystander usually declines and climbs down ladder. Repeat routine every Saturday and Sunday from 7:00 A.M. to 3:00 P.M.

I never climbed the ladder. I was too afraid. I still have no idea what the world's strangest animal looks like.

A similar routine happens in junior high ministry. Once or twice a week, junior high students gather together. Curious bystanders poke their heads into the junior high room to take a look at these

LISTEN UP!

"If one of the adult volunteers was thinking about quitting, I'd remind her that God didn't quit and she shouldn't either."

—Jen, eighth grade

strange animals. Curious bystanders are often shocked by what they see, which often results in a gasp or two. Operator of junior high ministry often asks if curious bystander would like to get involved. Curious bystander usually declines. Repeat routine every week.

Sadly, not enough people choose to get involved in junior high ministry. You won't find this book at the top of any bestseller lists (of course, you can change that by purchasing a copy for 100 of your closest friends). Of those who *do* get involved, few are committed to it long-term.

This saddens me because young teens, early adolescents, junior highers, middle schoolers, 12-14-year-olds—however you choose to describe them—are worth our time. I've spent the last thirteen years in full-time junior high ministry and hope to end my career working with junior highers because I think they're worth my time.

My friend Rick Williams has spent twenty years juggling his personal life, his family life and his professional life around junior high ministry because junior high students are worth his time.

THEY CAN BE:

annoying . . .
but they're worth his time.

immature . . .
but they're worth his time.

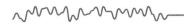
rude . . .
but they're worth his time.

insecure . . .
but they're worth his time.

mean . . .
but they're worth his time.

THEY ARE
loved by God . . .
and because of this, they're worth his time.

I don't know how long you intend to stay involved in junior high ministry, but I hope you'll stick around awhile. Junior high ministry deserves more than to be viewed as a steppingstone to "real" ministry. It deserves more than the reluctant mom who couldn't say no when asked to help out. It deserves more than the overprotective dad whose motives for involvement are wrong. Junior high ministry deserves adults who are committed for the long haul.

BRAINWAVES

Healthy ministry is the result of a healthy personal life.

I sat down with Rick Williams to discuss some of the keys to long-term junior high ministry. We discovered that long-term fulfillment requires attention to two arenas: the personal life and the ministry setting. Often these two arenas overlap and it can be difficult to separate them, but we tried. Let's take a look at some practical steps that can be taken to help you hang in there for the long haul. There is absolutely no research represented here, just two guys who have 33 years of junior high ministry combined, sharing their hearts.

LONG-TERM FULFILLMENT REQUIRES ATTENTION TO YOUR PERSONAL LIFE

Puffy, arrogant leaders don't last long.

Healthy, long-term ministry is a result of paying attention, first, to your personal life. Leaders with an unhealthy personal life eventually burn out, fizzle out, drop out or are asked to step out.

Appreciate your life stage.

In Philippians 4:12, Paul said,

"I know what it is to be in need, and I know what it is to have plenty. I have learned the secret of being content in any and every situation, whether well fed or hungry, whether living in plenty or in want."

Healthy leaders are content leaders. I don't know how old you are or if you're married or single. I don't know your financial situation or what you do for a living. Contentment doesn't come from what we have, but who we are. Paul understood that, in Christ, he had everything he needed. Long-term fulfillment comes from being content in the present.

Beware of pride.

"'. . . The person who wishes to boast should boast only of what the Lord has done'" (1 Corinthians 1:31, NLT).

We serve an awesome God! Everything we have accomplished and accumulated is because of his goodness. Remember that. Humility is a quality God favors; pride is one he detests. Puffy, arrogant leaders don't last long.

Create a dependence on God.

David said in Psalm 62:7, 8,

"My salvation and my honor depend on God; he is my mighty rock, my refuge. Trust in him at all times, O people; pour out your hearts to him, for God is our refuge."

You don't need to *create* a dependence on God. Everything that has and ever will exist is dependent upon God. You may, however, need to create the desire to live a life that recognizes your dependence on the Creator. Leaders who recognize their dependence on God desire to spend time with him, to listen to his voice, to follow his will, to read his Word, to sit at his feet. Your ability to *do* what God asks you to do relies on your willingness to *be* who he asks you to be.

Develop accountability.

Do you have someone in your life who holds your feet to the fire? Someone who asks you the tough questions like:

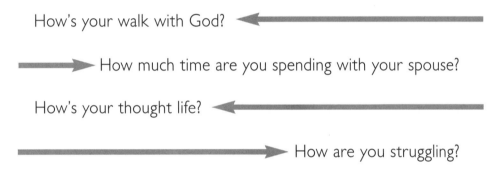

How's your walk with God?

How much time are you spending with your spouse?

How's your thought life?

How are you struggling?

You need someone in your life who knows you—the good you, the bad you and the ugly you—but loves you anyway. Someone who loves you enough to pray for you, encourage you and confront you when the need arises.

Experience personal growth.

In addition to growing spiritually (dependence on God), you need to be growing personally. Read books, subscribe to magazines, watch the Discovery Channel, take an additional college course, go on a nature hike. If all you do is read *Mad* magazine and watch MTV because you want to relate to students, you're in trouble. God gave Solomon incredible wisdom. You and I aren't so lucky!

Put family first.

If you're not married yet, you most likely will be someday. If you don't yet have children, that joy could very easily be in your future. Determine now that your future spouse and children will take priority over your ministry to students. Few things hurt my heart as much as seeing people neglect their family for the sake of ministry. My children's soccer games are more important than those of my students. Did you hear that? It's important that you really have a firm handle on this, because some people in your church might think your students' games are more important than those of your own kids.

BRAINWAVES

Don't sacrifice your own children in your attempt to minister to someone else's.

Time with my wife is more valuable than time with other volunteers. I like junior high ministry a lot. I like the business and fast-paced nature of what I do. I like it a lot—but I like my family a lot more! I demonstrate that by showing them how I set my priorities.

Get a life!

Every once in awhile someone will say to me, "Junior high ministry is my life!" What a sad statement! Please understand, I am committing a huge chunk of my life to minister to junior high students, but it's only part of my life. My life consists of hanging with my family, spending time with my friends, surfing, swinging at golf balls (once in awhile I actually hit one), going on vacation, laying around on my day off, going to late-night movies, taking the training wheels off my kids' bikes and a number of other things. I'm glad junior high ministry is on your list, but I hope it isn't the only thing on it.

I'm not a big advice giver, but let me give those of you who are young one piece of advice I had to learn the hard way: Develop healthy work habits and boundaries now because you don't want to try to develop them later. Churches love single people. Single people work long, hard hours. Single people volunteer for all kinds of stuff. Single people often allow ministry to take up unhealthy amounts of time. You may be able to get away with it now, but such habits will be hard to break later in life.

Hang out with nonministry friends.

You need friends who aren't involved in your ministry. Believe it or not, ministry friendships are often the most shallow. Think about it: when you're together, junior high ministry, students, families and other church issues inevitably find their way into the conversation. Because of this, ministry friendships have a hard time getting below surface level. Most of my close friends aren't involved in junior high ministry and aren't all that interested in it.

Invest in the kingdom.

I'm not talking about time. I'm talking about money. It's been said that the last thing to get saved is the wallet. If that's true, some of you reading this book are

Learn the art of saying no.

good Christians who are involved in good ministries but have yet to experience the joy that comes with regular giving. God blesses those who give. Selfishly holding back any area of our lives from God, including our finances, hurts our ability to persevere in ministry. If these statements have upset you, start giving—you'll feel much better.

Just say no.

You can't do it all. Not every good opportunity is a good opportunity for you. Decide what's important to you and neglect the things that aren't. Learn to say

Not every good opportunity is a good opportunity for you.

no. My pastor, Rick Warren, likes to say this: "He who burns the candle at both ends isn't as bright as he thinks he is."

LONG-TERM FULFILLMENT REQUIRES ATTENTION TO YOUR MINISTRY SETTING

I don't know how long you've been in your current ministry setting or how long you plan to stay. I hope you plan on staying until God tells you otherwise. Too often, people move out of a ministry or out of a church prematurely. Paying attention to a few things may help you persevere.

Appreciate where God's placed you.

God has you right where he wants you. I know your church isn't perfect; neither is mine, but it's where God wants you—at least for now. Instead of looking around for greener grass, water the grass you have! Besides, you may think the grass is greener on the other side of the fence, but when you get there you often discover it's AstroTurf! God has placed you in a unique church in a unique community and surrounded you with unique people to reach unique students. Make the most of the unique opportunity he's given you!

Be a team player.

Junior high ministry isn't the only ministry in your church. It may be the most godly ministry in the church, but it isn't the only one! What kind of reputation do you and your junior high ministry have? Are you viewed as selfish, complaining and unwilling to contribute to the overall efforts of the church? I hope not.

We share our meeting area with about five other ministries on a regular basis. It's a serious inconvenience for everyone. Often, as our junior high team is scrambling to tear down so the singles ministry can occupy the tent, I find myself grumbling.

Remembering that our junior high ministry is part of a larger team helps keep my attitude in check. It also helps my relationships with my other teammates.

HOW TO BE A TEAM PLAYER:

Take a look at the needs of other ministries in your church.

Express genuine interest in what they're up to.

Ask how you can help.

Make the time to follow through.

Communicate regularly with your supervisor.

Most of you answer to someone. It may be the youth pastor, the CE director, the parent committee, the elders or the senior pastor. I'm not sure who it is, but most likely someone else is ultimately responsible for your ministry to junior high students. Whoever supervises you needs to hear from you. He or she needs to hear when things are going well and when things aren't. Making an effort to keep your supervisor informed will gain trust and that trust is very important.

LISTEN UP!

"I really like most of the adults in our group, but there are a few that if they wanted to quit, I'd offer to pack their luggage."

—Jeff, eighth grade

Send short e-mails, drop a note in his box, send copies of your mailers. Make consistent attempts to keep him "in the know." If something goes wrong, it's better for your supervisor to hear about it from you than from someone else.

As I mentioned earlier, we left a junior high student at a football game . . . something went wrong. The dad was furious and he insisted on setting up a meeting with our executive pastor. As soon as I got home that night, guess what I did? I called our executive pastor and filled him in on the details. I didn't want him to be caught off guard by an irate parent. Communicating and admitting mistakes instead of trying to cover them up builds trust with your supervisor and helps ensure long-term ministry.

Don't compare.

Don't compare your church with the one down the street. Don't compare your budget to the children's ministry budget. Don't compare your junior high ministry to someone else's. Nothing good comes from comparing. Pride, envy, bitterness, justification and more are all that result.

Nothing good comes from comparing.

Enjoy the process.

I love this passage of Scripture from 1 Corinthians 3:6-10:

"I planted the seed, Apollos watered it, but God made it grow. So neither he who plants nor he who waters is anything, but only God, who makes things grow. The man who plants and the man who waters have one purpose, and each will be rewarded according to his own labor. For we are God's fellow workers; you are God's field, God's building. By the grace God has given me, I laid a foundation as an expert builder, and someone else is building on it. But each one should be careful how he builds."

In these verses the apostle Paul lays out what I like to call the "Process Principle." As a junior high worker, you are expected to play a part in God's process in the lives of students—he doesn't expect you to do it all. Not every student who walks through the doors of your ministry is going to head into high school as a fully committed, contagious Christian. Often, you are planting seeds

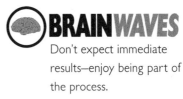

BRAINWAVES

Don't expect immediate results—enjoy being part of the process.

that will be watered over time and harvested at a later date.

I used to be frustrated by the fact that so many junior highers were seemingly slipping through God's hands. "Why can't our ministry get more kids saved?" I'd often think to myself. In recent years I've learned that it isn't the responsibility of my ministry to get every student saved—it's my responsibility to be part of the process.

I went to church in junior high, but didn't give my life to Christ until I was a junior in high school. Did the junior high department of my church fail me? Absolutely not! It succeeded in planting seeds of faith in my heart. It fulfilled its part of the process.

Don't expect immediate results—enjoy being part of the process. It will help you stick around awhile.

Fail forward.

I don't have the gift of prophecy, but I know this: You are going to make mistakes. Don't worry about failure; it comes with the territory. In my opinion, if you're not failing, you're not trying!

BRAINWAVES

Keep a journal of what you've learned from your mistakes.

The only time failure is failure is if you fail to learn from it. I don't mind making mistakes, but I don't want to make the same mistakes over and over again.

When you fail, be sure to pick yourself up, brush yourself off, learn from your mistakes and better yourself because of them. Your willingness to take risks adds value to your team. Failure comes with the territory. When you refuse to learn from mistakes and constantly repeat them, you become a liability.

Go for it!

Take a chance, try something new, create a twist in your ministry, use a new color paper for your handouts. Do something . . . anything! Your church may not fully understand junior high ministry, but people do expect to see junior high ministry taking place. That's why you're there. Mix things up a little. Remember, the purposes of the church stay the same but how you fulfill them is up for grabs. Use your creative skills (I've already proved you possess them) every once in awhile. Appropriate, thoughtful change can bring a sense of excitement to the group. Don't let boredom and the status quo push you out of junior high ministry.

Honor church traditions.

Including this piece of advice goes against my grain. It was my buddy Rick's idea. I guess after 20 years he's learned a few things. When I think of church traditions I think of old, outdated rituals that have little or no relevance to twenty-first century life. Actually, it doesn't matter how I feel about them. The fact is that church traditions exist and most of them aren't going away anytime soon, which is exactly what makes them traditions. Hymns were around long before you arrived on the scene and they will be there long after you're gone.

Revolting against sacred cows often results in a stampede.

For the first six years of my ministry, I served in a denomination that was very traditional. One tradition was that of not allowing dancing. A common joke among the younger ministers was that the reason our denomination was opposed to premarital sex was-because it could lead to dancing.

If your church is steeped in traditions, it would be wise to embrace them rather than revolt. Revolting against sacred cows often results in a stampede.

Obviously, many of our traditions could benefit from being reevaluated, but some of them are still of value. One benefit of church traditions is that they help students appreciate their Christian heritage. Another benefit is . . . is . . . is . . . sorry I can't think of another.

Invest in others.

If you want to stay in junior high ministry for the long haul, you must invest in others. In order to keep yourself from burning out, you need to share the load with others. It's wise, it's biblical and it's already been discussed in chapter two.

Juggle wisely.

Is it "Just say no," or is it "Juggle wisely"? It's both. The reason you must learn to say no is so there is room for those times when you can't. Part of being on a team is going the extra mile when needed. There are times when you will feel more like a circus juggler than a junior high worker. In these moments, be sure to juggle wisely.

Some tasks require lots of attention; others are low maintenance. Some tasks are emotionally draining; others may actually energize you. Junior high ministry requires the ability to juggle lots of stuff at once. It requires the ability to say no to some opportunities and yes to others. It requires the ability to juggle the tension between being a team player and looking out

LISTEN UP!

"I think it takes nerves of steel to work with us. . . . We can be pretty annoying."
—Miranda, seventh grade

for your own interests. It requires the ability to juggle ministry with family and personal time.

Junior high ministry is a lot like juggling chain saws: it's exciting, it requires a unique set of skills and very few are willing to try it. Junior high ministry is a juggling act . . . juggle wisely.

Not enough people choose to get involved in junior high ministry. Of those who do get involved, few are committed to it long-term. I hope you'll consider hanging in there for the long haul.

By the way, if you know what the world's strangest animal looks like, please let me know!

CHEW ON THIS

one Initially, what was your motivation for getting involved in junior high ministry?

two Has that motivation changed? If so, what keeps you involved now?

three Take another look at the "personal life" list. What areas need some extra attention in your life?

four Take another look at the "ministry setting" list. What areas need some extra attention in your ministry?

five

On a scale of 1 to 10, how likely is it that you'll stay involved in junior high for three years? Five years? Ten years?

1	2	3	4	5	6	7	8	9	10

CHAOTIC THOUGHTS

CHAPTER TEN

PARTING SHOTS

I've got a pet peeve. As I wander through Christian bookstores, browse exhibit halls at conferences and surf online, I'm frustrated by the fact that there simply aren't enough materials available for junior high workers. That frustration is largely responsible for my decision to write this book. I wanted to put one more resource in the hands of guys and gals who are in my boat—in love with junior high ministry and in need of encouragement.

I realize this book only begins to scratch the surface. To include every aspect of, and issue concerning junior high and middle school ministry would have demanded a five-hundred-page effort. I'm not the person to write such a book, and you're probably not the person to read it. After all, you do work with junior high students and sitting still long enough to read this book was probably challenging enough.

In an effort to cover a little more ground, I've created this short, A-Z list of tips and tidbits that may help you as you continue in your ministry to junior high students.

BRAINWAVES

Sooner or later, you *will* make someone upset.

Some of these may be little things that you already know; let them serve as reminders. Some of them may seem unreachable; give them a try anyway.

ANGRY PEOPLE

Sooner or later, you *will* make someone upset. When this happens, avoid the temptation to get defensive, even if you don't think the wrath is deserved. When talking to someone who's upset about an aspect of your ministry, you may want to employ the "Feel, Felt, Found" method.

Feel:
("I understand why you feel the way you do.")

Felt:
("In fact, others have felt the same way.")

Found:
("Here's what we've found. . . .")

BUDGET

If you're fortunate enough to be in a setting that designates funds for your ministry, here are a few thoughts:

Be good stewards: Don't spend foolishly. Keep good records.

Spend it: Spend your budget each year, or you'll likely see it cut.

Ask for more: Don't be afraid to ask for an increase every year or two. The worst they can say is no. Actually, they can say you're greedy, but at least you're greedy for a good cause!

CAMPUS PRESENCE

If your local school district allows you access to the campus, take advantage of it. Campus access tends to vary from district to district and often from school to school. Get to know administrators, and earn their trust by being interested in the big picture, not just your "Christian agenda." Even if they won't let you hold a campus Bible club, they'll likely let you coach a team, chaperone a dance or be a volunteer lunch aid.

BRAINWAVES

When asking for an increase in budget, be sure to detail how and where it will be spent.

BRAINWAVES

Earn the trust of school administrators by being interested in the whole picture, not just your agenda.

DEVELOPING LEADERS

Junior high is an ideal time to start developing leadership skills in students. The following are two possible approaches to take in developing student leaders:

Leadership by position

Students apply, interview and commit to the leadership team. In this approach, student leadership is a set group of students with set responsibilities and requirements. The leadership team meets regularly to plan, pray and prep the different aspects of the ministry. They have been given a position of leadership.

LISTENUP!

"The thing that encourages me most is a smile."
—Courtney, eighth grade

Leadership by influence

Adult volunteers begin to recognize the

175

influencers and provide miscellaneous opportunities for students to exercise their influence for the good of the group. In this setting, anyone can rise to leadership simply by virtue of influence.

E-MAIL

This is perhaps the single biggest advancement for youth ministry in the past twenty years. I take that back—the movement against "Chubby Bunny" is bigger, but e-mail's right up there. It's cheap, it's easy and it's still underused for the most part. Don't let e-mail replace the personal touch, but use it to keep parents, volunteers and students informed.

FINDING MORE HELP

In chapter two, we discussed what type of volunteers to look for and what roles they play. Another obvious question is, "Where do I find them?" For starters, you can talk to your local parole officer and see if he has anyone who needs community service. On second thought, it's probably best to start right where you are with who you have. The best place to find new leaders is by asking the leaders you currently have to spread the word.

BRAINWAVES
A simple misunderstanding can cause severe damage to your ministry.

Another idea is to ask your students to think of people in the church who they think would make good volunteers. You can have the students approach them or you can approach them by saying, "Brian thought you'd make a really good junior high volunteer. . . ." A third way to find new help is to ask your senior pastor to announce the need from the pulpit. The downside to this approach is that usually when a pastor asks for help, people come out of the woodwork to please him. That's not the motivation you want in a volunteer.

IRLS

If you are a guy, don't minister in a one-on-one setting with a girl. Don't give a girl a ride home. Don't step outside to counsel a girl. Don't, don't, don't! A simple misunderstanding or purposeful accusation of impropriety can cause severe damage to your ministry. If you're a female, take the same precautions when ministering to guys.

ELLO! . . . THOUGHTS ABOUT STARTING YOUR MEETINGS

The most important 20 minutes of any program are the ten minutes before you start and the ten minutes after you start. Pay extra attention to making the most of this crucial time. Here are a few tips:

 Greet students as they arrive.

 Introduce guests to regular attenders.

 Make sure adult and student leaders mingle with the masses.

 When possible, have junior-high-friendly music playing in the background.

"I don't think most adults realize that they really can make a difference in our lives."
—Blake, eighth grade

Do everything you can to create a warm, welcoming environment. When the time comes to start, start with enthusiasm, excitement and energy!

NCOME

If you get paid at all for doing what you do, it probably isn't much and it certainly isn't what you deserve. Because most youth workers aren't in the upper tax bracket, it's important to take advantage of the tax breaks you are given. You'll want to talk to your church administrator for more specifics, but here are two basic tips:

 Write stuff off: your mileage, lunches with students and those prizes you bought are usually deductible.

✓ If you're a licensed or ordained minister, you qualify for additional benefits. I can't go into all of them here, but they're well worth looking into.

UGGLING YOUR RESPONSIBILITIES

The wise junior high youth worker looks for ways to organize.

Organization is your friend. It takes a little extra effort on the front end, but it pays off. The only way to juggle your duties is to get aggressively organized. Buy a Daytimer or electronic organizer. One of my dad's favorite sayings when I was growing up was this: "Son, you never have time to do it right the first time, but you always seem to have time to do it over again." Organization will help you do it right the first time. In chapter nine, we discussed the importance of juggling wisely. Organization helps you juggle wisely and safely.

ISSING AND STUFF

"When should I kiss a boy?" "What's the right age to start dating?" "How far is too far?" I'm sure these questions sound familiar.

Hopefully these questions are coming from your students, not your adult volunteers! Most parents dodge these issues with their children and hope the church will tackle the issue for them. I wish that wasn't the case, but it is. Don't shy away from such discussions with your students; they are bombarded with a one-sided message and need to hear the truth from someone they trust. Consider teaching a three-week series on the subject that covers these topics:

"What Was God Thinking?"
(God's plan for sex)

"What Went Wrong?"
(How the world has twisted his plan)

"What's a Junior Higher to Do?"
(Pure living in an impure world)

LONERS

Be on the lookout for wallflowers. Better yet, ask students to be on the lookout. Most loners aren't loners by choice, but by chance. They just haven't been given a fair chance to break into the crowd. It's surprising how many seemingly shy, uninterested students are really chomping at the bit for a chance to participate, but they get overlooked. When you come across a student who likes being on the outside looking in, respect that. Slowly and gently encourage involvement, but never force it. It's better to have that student holding up a wall than to not have that student at all.

MIDDLE SCHOOL?

It's a tough issue with no easy answers. Most agree that sixth graders are a unique breed. I suggest you follow the lead of your community. If the schools in your district are made up of sixth to

 **BRAIN WAVES**

At the very least, help your church understand the uniqueness of sixth grade.

eighth grades, it makes sense that you would model your ministry appropriately in order to minister to your community. If the schools are seventh and eighth grade only, then you probably shouldn't rush sixth graders into your program.

Another approach I've used in the past, with surprisingly successful results, is to offer sixth-grade parents the option. Offer a sixth-grade ministry in the children's department, but also allow sixth graders to join in the middle school ministry. Let parents decide which option is best for their child. At the very least, help your church understand the uniqueness of sixth grade and that this age group deserves thoughtful attention.

N₀

Here are four ways to politely, yet firmly, say N . . . N . . . N . . . NO!

 "That sounds like a great opportunity, but I'm going to have to say no this time. Thanks for thinking of me."

 "Wow, that sounds great! I wish I could, but I can't."

 "That's just not something I'm going to be able to do this time."

 "I'm totally swamped. . . . Now get out of my face!"

ONCE

Be a risk taker! If it fits your purpose, try it. When trying something new, don't be afraid to let people know that it's just that . . . a trial. This way if it doesn't work out, you simply say, "Hey, we tried something new, but it didn't work." No big deal. I like the principle of "once." I'll try anything in our ministry once because we might stumble upon something special.

PERCEPTION

I could have, and probably should have devoted an entire chapter to this subject. Perhaps nothing has hurt junior high ministry more than its perception. We're unorganized, but wonder why we're not taken as seriously as other ministries. We dress and act like teenagers but wonder why we're not respected. The power of perception is incredible—don't underestimate it. What is perceived is believed.

BRAINWAVES
What is perceived is believed.

QUITTING

It's time to quit if God is moving you along. Don't quit out of frustration. Don't quit because your talk didn't go well on Sunday. Don't even quit because the parent committee is upset about the poop story you told at camp. Peaks and valleys are part of ministry. I hope you prayed about your decision to work with junior high students and did so because you felt it was where God wanted you. Don't quit until you've prayed about it and you're sure it's what God has in mind. If you do decide to move on, do so quickly. It isn't fair to students and other leaders to drag the process on unnecessarily.

LISTEN UP!
"Relax!"
—Matt, seventh grade

RULES

Don't be rule-happy. If there are tons of rules, you're probably the only one that's happy! We have one rule in our ministry: respect. Showing respect pretty much covers the bases. If I respect you, I'll treat you well. If I respect you, I won't steal your stuff. If I respect you, I'll listen to what you have to say, and so on. Doesn't respect have to be earned? Yes and no. Earned

BRAINWAVES

Don't be rule-happy.

respect is the most effective because it is voluntarily given. It is also effective as a rule: "In our ministry we will respect one another."

God gave the Israelites only Ten Commandments. Jesus narrowed those down to two. It seems funny to me that youth groups give students about 50.

SERIOUSLY

Some things need to be taken very seriously in your ministry. There are more, but let me list three:

ONE REPORTS OF ABUSE AND SUICIDE THREATS

You are legally required to report instances of physical and sexual abuse and suicide threats to the proper authorities. Talk to your church lawyer or senior pastor for a complete list of situations that require intervention.

TWO PARENTAL CONSENT FORMS

Don't leave the church property without them. When you take a student on an activity without consent, you are jeopardizing your church and yourself.

THREE INJURIES AND ILLNESS

Don't play doctor, even if you are one. If a student says he is sick or injured, call the parents. Let them decide the course of action to be pursued.

TEACHING TOPICS

Here is a list of ten series and a creative title for each one, just to get you started:

"Built to Last"
How to build a shake-proof faith

"Survival Kit"
The tools every Christian needs to survive

"Image Is Everything"
How to look good to God

"Open House"
How to make Christ at home in your heart

"Once Upon a Time"
Parables of Jesus

"Chew on This"
How to grow in Christ

"Time Machine"
How today's choices affect tomorrow

"He's the Man"
A look at the amazing life of Christ

"The Naked Truth"
Honest talk about love, sex and dating

"Make Your Mark"
How to make a lasting impression

UNDERWEAR

Stories that include underwear, boogers, poop, diapers, mucus, burps, phlegm and other such bodily functions will always catch the attention of a junior high student. Of course, they catch the attention of parents and the pastor too, but you can always tell them you were applying the "once principle" you read about in some lame book.

VALENTINE'S DAY

If you're married, do yourself a favor and tattoo February fourteenth along with your anniversary date on your arm. There should still be some room left under the Jesus tattoo. My point: Don't let ministry get in the way of what's really important.

BRAINWAVES

Don't let ministry get in the way of what's really important.

WEBSITES

Take advantage of the incredible technology that is at your fingertips. Spend time each week surfing the Web. Look at other ministries' sites to steal, I mean borrow, ideas. Browse the various youth ministry resource sites to find stuff that may not be available in stores. Sites can change their addresses quickly, so it's not worth listing them in this book. To get started, simply go to your favorite search engine and type in things like "youth ministry," "junior high ministry," or "ministry resources." The Youth Specialties website, www.youthspecialties.com, maintains a current list of links to helpful sites.

XYLOPHONE

This probably isn't an instrument too many junior high students play. It would be a cool addition to the worship team, though.

YOU ARE MAKING A DIFFERENCE

Really, you are! You may not always see it immediately; there are times when you won't see it at all. But your ministry to students is making a difference. Have a sower mentality. Enjoy being part of the process, God's plan for the lives of your students. Play your part with faithfulness, because your part is making a difference.

ZERO IN ON INDIVIDUALS

Junior high ministry is all about individuals. Don't let your programs, plans and purposes get in the way of seeing each student as a God-given opportunity. Instead, plan and program on purpose so that each individual God sends your way is valued as the incredible creation he or she is.

Put yourself in your students' shoes. Or better yet, put yourself back in your own.

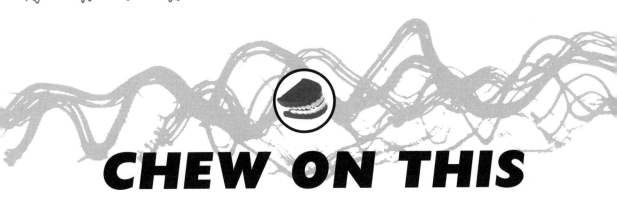

CHEW ON THIS

one How is your junior high ministry perceived by others in the church? What are some steps you can take to correct any misperceptions?

two What is one step you will take to help attract new leaders?

three Create a list of the five most influential students in your ministry. What are some extra opportunities you can give them to lead?

four Who are the students in your ministry that would most benefit from a little extra individual attention?

five On a scale of 1 to 10, how well do you play the xylophone?

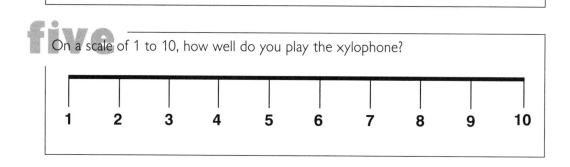

CHAOTIC THOUGHTS

ABOUT THE AUTHOR

Kurt Johnston has been a full-time junior high pastor since 1988, and he's still smiling! Currently, he is the junior high pastor at Saddleback Church in Lake Forest, California. Additionally, Kurt is the founder of Simply Junior High, an organization committed to encouraging junior high youth workers through resources and training. Kurt's desire is to stay involved in junior high ministry for the long haul and to help others to do the same.

Kurt lives in southern California with his wife Rachel and their two children, Kayla and Cole. In their free time, the Johnstons enjoy hanging out at the beach with their friends.

For more junior high resources by Kurt Johnston contact Simply Junior High at 949.766.1643 or visit www.simplyjuniorhigh.com.

Other EMPOWERED youth products
from Standard Publishing

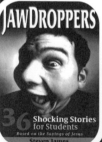